THE SASSY LADIES'
Toolkit for Start-up Businesses

Dear Karen —

THE SASSY LADIES'
Toolkit for Start-up Businesses

By
MICHELLE GIRASOLE,
WENDY HANSON,
and MIRIAM PERRY

Wishing you great
business success!

ANOTHER "SUCCESSFUL WOMEN IN BUSINESS" RESOURCE

Sassily Yours —
Wendy

Two Harbors Press
212 3rd Avenue North, Suite 290
Minneapolis, MN 55401
612.455.2293
www.TwoHarborsPress.com

ISBN - 978-1-935097-45-7
ISBN - 1-935097-45-8
LCCN - 2009922980

Book sales for North America and international:
Itasca Books, 3501 Highway 100 South, Suite 220
Minneapolis, MN 55416
Phone: 952.345.4488 (toll free 1.800.901.3480)
Fax: 952.920.0541; email to orders@itascabooks.com

Cover Design by Alan Pranke
Typeset by Peggy LeTrent

Printed in the United States of America

We dedicate this book to every woman who's ever wanted to be her own boss because, when you want a job done right, you gotta do it yourself.

TABLE OF CONTENTS

ACKNOWLEDGEMENTS

To Rich, Jessie, and Nicholas: If you had not given me the time and space to explore my own business, I would not be living the life of my dreams. I count my blessings daily to have your love. To Mom and Dad: Through your examples I learned how entrepreneurship can change one's life—for better and worse—and I consider your experience to be a far superior lesson in small business than my eight years of business school! But most of all, you taught me that family is what matters most, and any love and attention given to your family pays the highest dividends of all. To my other Mom and Dad, there is no doubt that I could not have done this without you both. Because of you, I was sure that my two cherubs were safe and happy while I was at work, and could fully concentrate on growing my business. You have no idea how much your gift has meant to me.

To Steve, Laura, Doug, Mary Ann, Erin, Wes, and all who have been involved with Precision Web Marketing: Thanks for letting me "practice" the concepts in this book with you over the last six years. It is clear that I don't have all the answers, but it is safe to say we've achieved an impressive level of success so far. With all of you, it has not felt like work.

To Miriam and Wendy: It is no accident that the three of us came together back in 2004 to work on Corley Hanson's e-mail campaign. I used to think the idea for the book was mine, but now I'm pretty convinced that it was Wendy's extensive vision for her perfect life that drew me in! By the grace of God, Miriam agreed to join the "project," and I'm excited about how far we've come. I celebrate the release of this book, our accomplishments to date, and our future success. We are just getting started!

—*Michelle Girasole*

This fabulous journey has really just begun. To Will, my husband and other business partner: Thank you for appreciating what brings me joy and always celebrating the vision of success for The Sassy Ladies. To my nieces—Amy, Chrisann, and Bridget—who exemplify smart and sassy young women who inspire me to "play big." With tears of joy, thank you to Miriam and Michelle, who always exceed my expectations of partnership, brilliant women, friends, and soul sistahs.

—*Wendy Hanson*

There is no greater gift in this life than the opportunity to make your dreams come true. And there is no task more enjoyable than thanking the people who got you there because it means a) your dream came true, and b) someone believed in you. Writing a book has been one of my lifelong dreams; I owe deep gratitude to my husband, Gene, who has never questioned whether I could do it, but only when I would. And to Michelle and Wendy, my soul sistahs, who found me when I needed finding. My cup runneth over.

—*Miriam Perry*

INTRODUCTION

We're The Sassy Ladies and we're here to help you make your dream of owning your own business come true. Now, we know there are dozens of books you could have bought, and maybe already own, that promise the same thing. So we thank you for trusting us to guide you on this new adventure of yours. Because that's what it is: an exciting quest! Ah, but we're getting ahead of ourselves (we get like that when we're excited).

Our book is unique in one very important way. We're going to give you the tools and resources, when you need them, at each step in the process of starting your own business. Now, there's a place for those other books; heaven knows we've used them ourselves. But this is a workbook to get your business from the dream stage to the oh-my-gosh-I'm-running-my-own-business stage. You'll find exercises, tips, and resources in every chapter. That means you've got some work ahead of you. But we're going to be there with you, not just in this book, but on our Web site (www.TheSassyLadies.com) and in our blog, supporting you every step of the way.

This is a good time to tell you just who The Sassy Ladies are. **Michelle Girasole** recently sold her partnership in Precision Web Marketing, and is an online marketing services expert. She has helped her clients, which range from female-owned start-ups to Fortune 500 companies, market their products and services online, using tools such as search engine marketing, permission-based e-mail, podcasting, blogging, and Web site analytics. Michelle regularly teaches workshops and seminars to entrepreneurs, businesspeople, and business school students. She helped launch a peer-to-peer business advisory board program for the Entrepreneurship Forum of New England. She received her master's degree in business administration and marketing degree from the University of Rhode Island. She is the mother of two young children and three old cats, and the wife of one handsome husband.

Wendy Hanson is a business coach and consultant. She co-founded Corley Hanson Associates in 1998, a coaching and leadership organization working with corporations around the country, including Google. Wendy has extensive experience coaching women in business. She owned a retail store, Wendy's Country Things and Herb Garden in Groton, Massachusetts, for three years. In her formal role as a special education administrator, she developed many businesses that provide training opportunities for people with disabilities. One of those businesses, Petalworks, produced potpourri from donated funeral flowers. The potpourri became part of a line of products for a national stationery and gift basket company. In 2004, Wendy was awarded the Women in Business Champion of the Year Award from the Small Business Administration in Rhode Island. Wendy has a master's degree in organization and management from Antioch New England and is a certified professional co-active coach from the Coaches Training Institute.

Miriam Perry develops effective business and marketing communications for companies in the corporate and non-profit sectors. Whether developing and implementing a full-scale strategic communication plan for a new employee program, evaluating materials to ensure they meet their objective, or writing a case study, Miriam provides solutions that ensure the right message is not only produced, but received by its intended audience. Her clients and employers have included Bryant University, Blue Cross Blue Shield Rhode Island, FM Global, Fidelity Investments, and Mayo Clinic. Miriam gets a kick out of the fact that she can make a good living doing what she loves the most: writing. Before her lifelong dream of being a published and paid writer came true, she was a member of the United States Air Force. That's where she learned to Aim High! and fold her T-shirts into perfect, six-inch squares; the former has been very useful in making her dreams come true, the latter not so much.

But it's not just our experiences you'll benefit from in this book. We've talked to other women who want to share their knowledge with you. Learn from them. They know what they're talking about. We present all of this wisdom in a casual, easy-to-read style. And yes, we live up to our name and can be quite sassy. We don't take ourselves too seriously, we won't let you off the hook, and we love to laugh. But don't let our lightheartedness fool you. We are completely serious about providing you with practical wisdom you can start using right now to get your business up and soaring.

WHOM THIS BOOK IS FOR
This book is for you if you are:
- Thinking about starting your own business.
- In the process of starting your own business.
- Already in business, but want to be sure you've covered the basics.
- The owner of a franchise or multi-level business, such as Arbonne, The Pampered Chef, etc.

While many of these types of organizations do provide marketing and business guidance, it never hurts to supplement that knowledge.

WHO ARE YOU?
We love meeting the many women who have felt the call to entrepreneurship. You inspire us, keep us real, make us laugh, and never fail to show us a new thing or two. Love that. Come to the blog on our Web site (www.TheSassyLadies.com) and introduce yourself.

HOW TO MAKE THE MOST OF THIS BOOK
In the main section of each chapter, you'll find:

In Her Words
Here's your chance to walk in another woman's pumps. These are excerpts from our interviews with women who are in various stages of running their own businesses. Whether in their first year or their tenth, you can glean a lot of wisdom from their experiences. Listen to the full interviews on our Web site.

The Sassy Ladies Say
Each of us—Michelle, Wendy, and Miriam—brings a different perspective to the topics in this book and this is where you hear it straight from our sassy little mouths.

Exercises

You can read about doing something and never actually get anything done. This is a working book. The exercises we've provided here will walk you through the steps you have to take to get your business up and running. Sure, you could skip them, but we promise they are worth the effort.

We suggest you copy the exercises and tuck them into your purse so you can make good use of downtime when waiting in the doctor's office or in line at the grocery store.

Bright Ideas

These are simple tips related to the information provided in a particular section.

At the end of each chapter, you'll find:

Reflections

One of the best ways to capture new knowledge is to rephrase it in your own words. Writing about what you've just learned is an effective way to do this.

Coaching

Professional athletes have them, corporate executives have them, and now you, too, can benefit from having a coach. These exercises will not only motivate you; they help you take the action you need to start or grow your business.

Toolkit

There is no need to go this alone or to reinvent the wheel. Take advantage of the resources available to you. We've provided you with a good start. In some cases, the items in the toolkit build on the knowledge in the chapter; other items offer inspiration to feed your enthusiasm and your entrepreneurial spirit.

Each chapter focuses on a different topic of how to be successful in your first year of business. You may want to go through each chapter in the order we suggest or you may start with the one that suits your current situation. Unlike ponchos and leg warmers, getting your business up to speed is not one-size-fits-all. This diagram shows the different steps needed in your first year of business and it's how we've structured this book, but remember: However you choose to make the journey is the right way for you.

CHAPTER ONE

DREAMING ABOUT YOUR BUSINESS

"One must desire something to be alive."
—Margaret Deland (1857-1945), American novelist

In this chapter, you'll learn how to:
- Start to make your dream a reality.
- Turn negative self-talk into positive encouragement.
- Get inspired.

This dreaming chapter is an effective first step in getting your business started. Some of us spend months, even years, thinking, "Some day I'll have my own business," but never actually make it happen. That's because that first step is a doozy, and it can be tough to take. This chapter will make it easier by helping you make your dream real. If you think of your first year in business as a journey, then this is the part where you decide where you want to go. Even if you've jumped into your business without spending too much time dreaming about it, you might find it useful to step back for a moment and use the information and exercises in this chapter. Think of it as a reality check to be certain you're doing what's really important to you.

Perhaps you know someone who is living her dream. That person lives with a sense of purpose, filling each day with whatever is important to her. She has a sense of balance, accomplishment, and daily joy. You know the type. You can choose to envy her, or let her inspire you to live your dream. You also have a dream. It's about being independent, financially free, successful, or famous. Maybe it's about giving back to your community or making the world a better place. Or, it's about _____ (fill in the blank). In this dream, you see yourself doing what you love and loving what you do. You're filled with a sense of satisfaction, happiness, and confidence. Hold that thought.

To turn your dream into a profitable business, you have a lot of practical steps ahead of you, some that are not as fun as the fantasy you've created in your mind's eye. That's why it's so important to hold on to the dream to motivate and sustain you. Too often, we talk ourselves out of our dreams (or worse, we let others do that) because we don't have enough time, money, experience, connections, _____

_____

(fill in your usual excuse here). If you're reading this book, you've moved past the vague, squishy, "If I ever win the lottery, I'll ..." stage and have decided to take action toward starting your own business. Congratulations! You've reached an important milestone in your life. This is when you've decided you're going to live your life on your terms. It may be a risk, but in your heart, you know it's an even bigger risk not to do it.

In Her Words

"I was almost crippled with fear about starting my business because it was such a big undertaking. I was waiting for a man to lead me. I was waiting for someone with experience to lead me. But what I realized was that there is nothing you can't do from where you stand today. My advice to you is, 'Yes, you can!'"

—Michelle B. Davidson, President, Trinity Mortgage Solutions
(www.TrinityMortgageOnline.com)

Hear our full interview with Michelle on our Web site. We think Michelle's courage and determination are all the more inspiring when we consider that she was only 29 when she started her business!

DEFINE YOUR DREAM

You have to define your dream before you can achieve it. You may be one of the lucky ones who knows exactly what you want to do. You may already know that if you don't try to sell your handmade cards, you won't be able to sleep at night. But you may not be that sure. Your dream may be less about what you do than what having your own business allows you to do: make more money, spend more time with your family, or travel. So your first step is to describe what your heart's desire is.

Still not quite sure what your dream is? Think about the values that are most important to you. Knowing which values you hold dearest will help you make meaningful choices as you start and sustain your business. According to Wikipedia.org, values are "principles, standards or qualities considered worthwhile or desirable by the person who holds them." The following values exercise will help you identify the values that will serve as your guideposts for your business—and your life.

Values

Review the list of values below. First, pick ten values that resonate with you. From those ten, choose the three that are so important to you that you can't live without them. Keep in mind that values represent consistent behavior in different circumstances. Acting once or twice in a particular way does not indicate a value.

Accomplishment	Excellence	Learning
Acknowledgement	Flexibility	Lightness
Adventure	Free spirit	Mastery
Aesthetics	Freedom	Meaningful work
Altruism	Friendships	Participation
Appearance	Fun	Partnership
Authenticity	Growth	Pleasure
Beauty	Harmony	Privacy (solitude)
Commitment to goals	Home life	Productivity
Community	Honesty	Recognition
Compassion	Humor	Relationships
Comradeship	Independence	Risk taking
Cooperation	Influence	Self-expression
Creativity	Initiative	Spirituality
Directness	Inspiration	Stability
Discovery	Integrity	Success
Ease	Joy	Support
Elegance	Laughter	Teamwork
Empowerment	Lack of pretense	Winning
		Wisdom

With the three values you've just identified in mind, consider a situation in which you felt fulfilled, successful, and good about your life and your place in it. How were you honoring those three values?

Think about a time when you were unhappy and felt at odds with a situation. How were your most important values not being honored? Now think about how your business dream will align with your values.

For example, if you chose home life as one of your top three values, then a business that has you traveling two weeks every month might not be a good fit for you. If you chose elegance as a top value, then being a professional pooper scooper would hardly fit your desired lifestyle, either. You get the picture.

KEEP YOUR EYES—AND YOUR HEART—ON THE PRIZE

Remember how your mother would save her nice things for special occasions? The fancy china dishes, heirloom jewelry, and snazziest outfits would be "saved" for extraordinary days. What a shame to let those treasures get dusty and go unused. This will not happen to your dream! Take your dream out of the dark, dust it off, and show it off every day. That's how you make a dream a reality. (And while you're at it, wear your great-grandmother's diamond ring to go grocery shopping. Picking out peaches has never been so much fun. Eat your breakfast oatmeal out of your best china bowl. The oatmeal is good for your heart and enjoying one of your prized possessions is good for your soul.)

What's your business idea? Visualize it happening: see yourself running your own business. Say it out loud. Write it down. How does it make you feel? What makes it so interesting? So fulfilling? What impact would it have on your life?

Bright Idea Maybe you have a few dreams, components of a lifestyle your new business would make possible. Glue pictures representing those dreams to a piece of paper. Frame or laminate your dream collage and put it on your desk or wall so you can start each day with a reminder of the most important goal in your life right now. Remember: nothing is too extravagant or too out of reach. This is your dream!

THINK HAPPY THOUGHTS

One of the toughest people to convince that your business idea is possible is … you! No one can talk you out of something faster than you can. Self-talk can be defeating—or empowering. Choose to make it work for you by telling yourself what you can do. Whenever you have a negative thought, replace it with a positive one. Because we're much better at telling ourselves the bad news, here are some examples to get you positively talking to yourself.

Instead of this...	Think this:
I'm scared.	I am excited about this new adventure.
I will probably fail.	I will try my best.
I'm not smart enough.	I can learn.
I've never done anything like this before.	There's no time like the present to try something new.
I can't do this.	I am excited about this new adventure.
I don't have enough time.	I can manage my time better.

At this point, don't quit your day job, mortgage your house, or make drastic changes in your life; simply give yourself license to explore your idea to see if you can make it fly. And, if you have already done one or more of these things, then keep on reading, because there is no turning back!

SAY IT'S SO

Tell someone else about your dream. This is important for three reasons:

- When you tell someone your dream, you make it more real. It's no longer a private conversation. The act of putting your goal into words is empowering.
- Telling someone is a commitment, and once you've told someone you're going to do something, it's tougher to back out.
- You never know how someone can help you. One thing we know — you will always move ahead at a faster pace if you have a network of people to support you.

───────── **Sassy Idea** ─────────

Have a Dream Party

Our entrepreneurial friend, Tara Sage Steeves, is founder and president of Create Your Life!, LLC and The Dream Party™. Tara, life coach and expert on dream realization, invited attendees of her dream party to come dressed or decorated as they aspired to be in five years. A few came dressed as adventurers, wearing safari hats and hiking boots, ready to travel the world. One man carried the book he dreamed of writing. During this event, people declared their dreams and were introduced to people who could help them achieve them.

There were real estate agents for the dream home, travel agents for the dream vacation, entrepreneurial coaches for the dream business. During the event, Tara encouraged people to talk to each other about their dreams, and even sit inside an artist's rendition of a time machine to write down what they would be doing on that day, five years into the future. The whole evening was cheerful, fun, and inspiring, and many dreams were launched that night.

Tara Sage Steeves is the author of Are You Pregnant with a Dream? *Learn more on her Web site, www.CreateYourLifeInc.com, and contact Tara for licensing information about Dream Parties. Hear our interview with Tara on our Web site.*

THE LAW OF ATTRACTION

There's a belief that if you tell the Universe what you need, higher powers will work to answer that call. This ancient wisdom is called The Law of Attraction. Whether you believe in God, Buddha, Allah, Goddess, or the power of meditation, you can harness the energy of The Law of Attraction by stating intentions that will move you toward your goals. You can light a candle at the beginning of the day or simply form your intention in your mind while you brush your teeth. Whatever resonates with you is the right way.

Examples of intentions:
- My business is so successful I have replaced my current salary within the first six months.
- My business allows me to spend more time with my kids.
- My business provides me such a good living that I joyfully donate 10% of my profits to charity.

ACCENTUATE THE POSITIVE

Naysayers. Dream killers. Wet blankets. You know who they are. They
can summon a rain cloud on a blue-sky day faster than you can say,
"Don't ruin it for me!" You can't change them, so don't waste the energy. Instead, limit your contact with these parade-rainers. Now, if you
happen to live with one (or, yikes!, more than one), you can't avoid
him or her altogether. Just be judicious about what you share with this
person. When you have a new idea, go to someone with a more positive
outlook first. This will not only build your confidence, it will give you
the opportunity to consider some of the negative aspects of your idea
so that you're prepared to deal with the cynic. In fact, the pessimistic
people in your life can serve a useful purpose when you're ready to
consider the potential pitfalls of an idea.

As you go through the process of developing your new business,
you will come across successful, positive, supportive people in whose
company you shine. You know you've met these special people when
you walk away from them feeling ridiculously happy, confident, and
ready for action. Be sure to see these people on a regular basis to feed
you the positive energy to make your dreams come true. These are
important role models for you—watch how these people interact with
others, listen to how they speak about themselves and about others. In
short, learn from them.

Sassy Lady Michelle Says

My career plan upon graduating college was to pick up some job experience, hone my business skills, then start my dream company after five years or so, just in time to start a family. This would give me the balance I could never have working 50+ hours a week in corporate America. Once my husband and I got married and bought a house, however, it was really hard to give up my salary to start a risky venture. My husband was never very supportive when I spoke of my plans. He had a lot to lose and would have to agree to be the sole provider for our family for a while.

After the 9/11 terrorist attacks, the high-tech company I was working for lost promised funding and had to cut down its workforce—my job included. Plus, I was four-and-a-half-months pregnant. I remember calling a friend on the way home to tell her I had lost my job; she sounded so worried for me. She was surprised to learn how excited I was about it. Now we had no choice. My risky venture was now a viable income option and I was optimistic that Rich would no longer put up an argument! (He didn't, much to my delight.)

It is a scary thing to leave behind the stability and security of a good job. When your family depends on your income, it's a decision you cannot make alone. This is probably why many businesses are started when the owner is in transition (a divorce, a pregnancy, a move or death, etc.).

A QUICK WRAP-UP

Your dream—it's starting to feel real now, isn't it? It's no longer something that you keep to yourself, like a secret or the last piece of chocolate. No, this dream of yours to own your business is becoming a reality and it's time to make it known. You're in a good place, our Sassy Friend. Enjoy this moment!

REFLECTIONS

What are three things you're taking away from this chapter?

1. _____
   _____
   _____

2. _____
   _____
   _____

3. _____
   _____
   _____

COACHING FOR SUCCESS

As you define your dream, answer the following:

- When do I experience the most joy? How can that be part of my business?

   _____
   _____
   _____
   _____
   _____
   _____

- What do I want out of my business?

   _____
   _____
   _____
   _____
   _____
   _____

- What is the next small step I can take toward defining my dream?

   _____
   _____
   _____
   _____
   _____
   _____

TOOLKIT

Here are a few resources to feed your dreams.

Books

- *Excuse Me, Your Life Is Waiting: The Astonishing Power of Feelings* by Lynn Grabhorn describes the principles of the Law of Attraction. It is written with humor and includes great stories.
- *Soul Proprietor: 100 Lessons from a Lifestyle Entrepreneur* by Jane Pollak. "A primer on the daily lessons that business ownership teaches, this book explores how to maintain a balanced and joyful life while striking out on an entrepreneurial mission. Illustrates that structuring a business to reflect personal values is the true key to success." (Description from Amazon.com.)
- *Are You Pregnant with a Dream? Birthing a Dream: Conception to Age 5* by Tara Steeves. Through reflective exercises and thought-provoking questions, this book is a powerful resource to guide you through the process of unlocking your inner wisdom and revealing your dreams to the world, one easy step at a time.
- *Life Lessons for Mastering the Law of Attraction: Seven Essential Ingredients for Living a Prosperous Life* by Jack Canfield, Jeanna Gabellini, and Eva Gregory. Jeanna Gabellini and Eva Gregory are master coaches and experts in the Law of Attraction. Together with one of the superstar contributors to *The Secret*, Jack Canfield, they share powerful, life-changing lessons and techniques of the Law of Attraction.

Magazines

Get a monthly dose of business inspiration.

- *Inc.* This is the American entrepreneur's handbook. A one-year subscription includes 12 issues for $10. Web site: www.inc.com.
- *Entrepreneur* offers solutions for growing businesses. A one-year subscription delivers 12 issues for $15.97. Web site: www.entrepreneur.com.

Article

- "The Brand Called You," an online article at www.fastcompany.com/online/10/brandyou.html. As the CEO of You, Inc., it's up to you to determine what makes you unique, what you do that adds value to your employer or customer, and then promote that brand to create the future you want.

Movies

- *What The Bleep Do We Know!?* As with any endeavor in life—be it your business, your relationships, or your personal goals—the power of your thoughts cannot be underestimated. In this film, the science behind that connection is conveyed through lively, animated, and often humorous renditions of brain chemicals and other special effects.
- *The Secret* Learn about the force known as the Law of Attraction directly from philosophers, scientists, and authors; focus your thoughts to create your dream and turn it into reality.
- *The Journey* Listening in on Eric Saperston's conversations with celebrities and business leaders as the new college graduate follows The Grateful Dead on tour offers clarity into what's important in life: happiness, success, and more.

THE SASSY LADIES' WEB SITE RESOURCES

To show our appreciation for buying our book, we're providing you access to two additional resources, free of charge, on our Web site at www.TheSassyLadies.com/StartupChapter1.

- *30-Day Guide to Focus and Fulfillment in Your Business*—a journal you can print from our Web site to begin each day with purpose.
- *Creating Your Future* (audio)—In about five minutes, this guided meditation will help you envision the future you want to create.

Enjoy!

CHAPTER TWO

DETERMINING THE FEASIBILITY OF YOUR BUSINESS

"Learn from the mistakes of others. You can't live long enough to make them all yourself."
—Eleanor Roosevelt (1884-1962), U.S. diplomat

In this chapter, you'll learn how to:
- Identify who your customers are.
- Research your competition.
- Set your price.
- Put negative criticism to good use.
- Test your business idea.

Once you've given your business idea wings (which you did in the first chapter), you need to make sure it can really get off the ground. This chapter will help you lift off. If you think of your first year in business as a journey, then this is the part where you decide whether you have the right vehicle. Even if you've jumped into your business without spending too much time determining its feasibility, you might find it useful to step back for a moment and use the information and exercises in this chapter. Think of it as a reality check to be certain you're setting yourself up for success.

It's time to find out how *feasible* your business idea is. Feasible means how likely it is to be successful. In this stage of starting your own business you have to find out what the likelihood is that your idea will be everything you hope it will be. While it's important to do what you love, it's even more important that others love what you do enough to keep you in business. You have to align your passion and talents to the market and your customers' needs.

It's nice to think that everyone in the world will need and want your product or service, but it's more realistic to consider the group of people who are most likely to buy from you. Let's face it, chocolate-covered strawberries may be one of the most delicious treats in the world, but some people are allergic to strawberries. A housecleaning service seems like a godsend, but many people's budgets don't allow for it. The

13

key is to think about the words "most likely" to narrow your focus. By doing this, you'll identify your prospective customers. Marketers refer to this as your *target audience*.

Exercise

Define Your Audience

The following questions will help you define your audience. You'll notice we use the phrase "most likely" quite often. That's to remind you to think in general terms so you'll end up with a realistic profile of your customer. For example, while there are men who use skin care products, the primary market is women.

- Audience—Is your business geared mostly to individual consumers or businesses?
- If you're going to target primarily businesses, what size company would most likely buy from you based on your pricing structure? Who within the company would make the purchase decision?
- Purpose—Why do people need what your business offers?
- Gender—Are your customers more likely to be men or women?
- Age—What age group is most likely to want or need your offerings?
- Location—Is there a geographical area that is more appropriate than others? Do you have to consider geographical boundaries?
- Seasonal—Is there a time of year that is best suited to your product or service?

Once you've answered these questions, ask yourself: What am I taking away from this exercise? Where will my focus be?

KNOW YOUR COMPETITION

There's a good chance that somewhere, someone is running a business doing exactly what you want to do. In fact, there may be hundreds of similar businesses in your city. Should you give up? Absolutely not! Competition is a good sign; it means there's a need for your product or service. If someone else is making money from selling something similar, it confirms the need exists. You have to do a little bit of homework, though, to find out how much of a need.

You can learn a lot from your competitor's success as well as her failure: whether you need to tweak your idea by adding more of one thing or subtracting another, and whether you need to specialize or generalize. The following are several ways to find out who your competition is and how they're doing. Capture the information you collect in the following chart.

COMPETITOR MATRIX

Use this chart to list characteristics of your competitors in a convenient, at-a-glance format.

Competitor name and Web site	Business location	Price structure	Specialization/ niche	Comments, such as what you want to remember most about this business

HARNESS THE POWER OF THE INTERNET

Use an Internet search engine such as Google or Yahoo! to find your competition. If you don't find many relevant results, try several different phrases. For example, to find other party planners, search for: party planner, party planning, special events, and special event planning. Complete the following exercise as you review each site.

Exercise **Competitor Analysis**

Follow these steps to conduct an analysis of your competitors' Web sites.

1. How does your competitor describe her business on her Web site? Is it similar to how you see your business or do you see an opportunity to be different?
    *   What types of companies are listed in the client section (e.g., small businesses, Fortune 500 corporations, non-profit organizations, etc.)?
    *   If customer testimonials are published, notice what characteristics are being praised (e.g., speed, price, quality, creativity, professionalism, etc.). This can help you decide what your selling points should be.
    *   What's your overall impression of the business judging by the Web site: professional, amateurish, serious, cutesy, etc.?
    *   Read the news announcements. You'll find out what changes your competitor is making to her offerings, which can be a clue about where the market is heading.
2. If your competitor publishes a newsletter, sign up for it. You can get even more detail about the products and services she offers, her pricing, and more.
3. Bookmark the Web sites you like the most—and least—because you may want to refer to them again.

Once you've learned the above information, you can continue your research.

CALL

You may be surprised at how willing people are to share their experiences, even if you're a potential competitor. For one thing, a party planner in San Francisco, California, will probably not worry about you taking her business if you're starting the same business in Newport, Rhode Island. Plus, there really is room in the world for everyone. Most businesses have a niche, or specialty. For example, some communication professionals specialize in public relations while others focus on employee communications—two very different areas of expertise.

ASK YOUR COMPETITOR

- What has your biggest challenge been?
- What surprised you most about this business?
- What was the one thing no one ever told you that you wish they had?
- If you had to do it over again, what would you do differently?
- What important question haven't I asked you?

BE A MYSTERY SHOPPER

If you can, pose as a customer of your potential competitor. Buy her product or service and compare it to your own.

- What can you learn from it?
- How can you do better?
- Or, how can you establish a niche?

A Sassy Lesson

A friend of ours, Rochelle, considered starting a custom scrapbooking business. To research the feasibility of her idea, she searched the Internet for Web sites that offered similar services. Rochelle not only discovered scrapbook services she hadn't considered, but found the prices were much higher than she was planning to charge. When she spoke with a potential customer about her idea, the woman gave Rochelle yet another idea for a product line and, surprisingly, told her that her pricing was too low; she would expect to pay much more for Rochelle's services. When Rochelle is ready to launch her new business, she's now confident she'll be offering products her customers want, and she has set her prices appropriately.

WHY ARE YOU SO SPECIAL?

This is not a challenge. It's a real question, aimed at getting you to think about what it is that makes your business, well, your business. Marketers call this your unique selling proposition, or USP. A company's USP is often in its tagline.

- FedEx's tagline and USP once was: When your package positively, absolutely has to be there overnight.
- The Home Depot: You can do it, we can help.
- Southwest Airlines: You are now free to move around the country.

When you can focus your business this tightly, you've established why your customers need you. Just remember that the point of developing your USP isn't to have a snazzy tagline, though if it works out that way, great. Concentrate on defining your business.

DEVELOP YOUR ELEVATOR PITCH

When you introduce yourself to someone, you should be able to tell that person what you do in the time it takes you to take an elevator ride—hence the term *elevator pitch*. This is an essential skill to practice. It should take you no more than ten seconds to describe your business. Any longer than that and you risk losing that person's attention. Plus, if it takes you two minutes to explain what you do, it's a sign you may need to refine your focus.

To craft your elevator pitch, answer the following questions: what, who, when, where, why, how. Here's an example of our elevator pitches for our three individual businesses:

The Sassy Ladies Say

Michelle: Precision Web Marketing provides online marketing strategy and services to help companies use their Web sites to connect with customers on the Internet.

Wendy: Corley Hanson Associates is an executive coaching and leadership organization—we make your business a team sport!

Miriam: I develop business and marketing communications for internal and external audiences for companies of all sizes.

SETTING YOUR PRICES

Set your price too high and you won't get enough customers. Set it too low and you won't make enough money to cover your costs. Finding the right price for your product or service may seem like magic, but it really is a lot easier than pulling a bunny out of a hat. The trick is to know what the market value is and your audience's perception of the value of what you're selling.

The following guidelines to follow for retail and service pricing provide a basic framework; see the resources at the end of the chapter for more detailed formulas.

Product pricing structure

To figure out the price of your product, list the costs that go into the development and distribution of that product.

- Fixed costs—these are overhead expenses you pay for regardless of how much product you're producing. Examples: Web site hosting, networking fees, insurance, etc. (See Appendix A for a worksheet to list all of your costs.)

- Variable costs—expenses that depend on how much product you're creating fall into this category. Examples: raw material, packaging, shipping, etc.

Let's say you're selling homemade scarves online. Here's one way to determine if your price will cover your costs and make you a profit.

1. Calculate how much it costs to make a scarf (be sure to include only your variable costs).
2. Begin with a markup percentage (your profit percentage after expenses).
3. Using the final cost of the scarf as a baseline, figure out how many scarves you'd have to make in one month to cover your overhead expenses.

Example:

Cost to make one scarf	$12.00
Multiply by markup percentage	X33%
Markup amount	$4.00
Add markup amount to cost of scarf	$16.00
Total amount of fixed or overhead costs	$1550/month
Number of scarves you'd have to make to cover your costs and make a profit.	97

If you now see you'd have to make 97 scarves per month to cover your overhead expenses and make a $4 profit per scarf, the question to ask yourself is, "Self, can I make 97 scarves every month? And if I can, will I be able to live on this projected income? Is it enough to pay my bills, take a yearly vacation, and afford my custom-made Italian leather shoe habit?"

If it isn't feasible for you to produce 97 scarves in a month or make a living on these numbers, consider increasing the price of your scarves or develop other ways to create revenue around this idea: teaching scarf-making classes or producing a kit with instructions on how to make a scarf.

Service pricing structure

When you offer a service such as consulting, accounting, marketing, etc., you're charging for your time rather than a physical object. In this case, you're concerned with billable hours: that is, how many hours you can bill a client in a given day, week, month, or year.

When you work for someone else and get paid an annual salary, you're getting paid for 52 weeks a year, 40 hours a week (that's 2,080 hours per year). But when you work for yourself, you have to account for the hours in the week you aren't billing clients: time spent on administrative tasks (record keeping, adding contact info to your address book, etc.), marketing yourself (attending networking meetings, for example), and more. On average, a realistic estimate is that you'll work a maximum of 1,132 billable hours. Don't misunderstand: when you run your own business, you'll work far more than that, but your billable hours are what help determine your pricing.

Setting your rates isn't as easy as using the salary or hourly rates you made when you were working for someone else as a basis. If you have to pay for medical and other benefits, you'll have to account for those costs. You also have to consider the cost of running a business.

The following is one way to determine your rates.* Before you begin, you must first know your expenses. A worksheet is provided in Appendix A to help you identify your expenses. Let's use an example with $48,000 of expenses.

1. Determine billable days
   a. Begin with standard work hours available per year = 2,080 hours
   b. Deduct vacation (10 days), sick time (5 days), holidays (9 days)
      24 days x 8 hours = 192 hours
      2,080 hours-192 = 1,888 hours
   c. Deduct administrative, marketing, education, etc. = 40% of remaining hours
      40% of 1,888 hours = 756 hours
   d. Total billable hours = 1,888-756 = 1,132 hours (which amounts to 141 days per year)
2. Determine costs, including overhead
   a. Divide total expenses by 141 days
      ($48,000 ÷ 141 = $340/day)
   b. Divide $340/day by 8 hours = $42.50 per hour. This is your *overhead rate.*
3. Determine labor rate
   How much do you want to make? Let's say $40,000/year.
   a. Divide $40,000 by 141 days = $284/day
   b. Divide $284/day by 8 hours = $35.50/hour. This is your *labor rate.*
4. Determine profit

a. Add overhead and labor rates ($42.50 + 35.50 = $78)

b. Take 20% of that number to find your *profit rate*.

5. Determine final billing rate

a. Add overhead, labor, and profit: $42.50 + $35.50 + $15.60 = $93.60/hour. This is your billing rate.

*From the Center for Women & Enterprise, Rhode Island

Whether you are selling a product or a service, the big question is the same: Will your customers pay that rate? You can find out if yours is close to the going rate by:

- Finding out what your competition charges, as described in the previous section.
- Checking out your industry's associations, which sometimes offer rate ranges depending on experience and geographical location. Association Web sites sometimes also have forums, where you can ask people for a realistic range. For example, *Writer's Digest* magazine publishes an annual survey of freelance rates for everything from advertising copy to Web site content.
- Asking for it. If your customers repeatedly reject your bid because of price, you know it's too high. On the other hand, if they don't hesitate, you may not be asking enough!

EARN TOP DOLLAR

Some people set their prices low to attract customers or break into a market. There are several reasons why this is a bad idea.

- **Worth**—If you feel the only way you're going to convince people to buy from you is to offer rock-bottom prices, the problem isn't a business issue; you need to boost your self-esteem. Tell yourself you're worth it—and believe it.
- **Value**—People perceive low cost as low value. If your prices are much lower than your competition, your prospective customers will think it's because you're not as good as your rivals.
- **Price increases**—At some point, you're going to have to raise your prices to cover your costs. Customers don't take well to price increases so you want to do this only when necessary.
- **Profit cushion**—Unexpected costs or downtime can be absorbed by a higher profit rate.
- **Flexibility**—You may want to give friends, family, and good customers a discount. Higher pricing gives you the flexibility to make those decisions.

WHAT TO DO IF YOUR PRICE SEEMS TO BE TOO HIGH

You've done your research, you know what your product or service is worth, yet either potential customers have told you you're too pricey or that's the conclusion you've come to. Before you lower your prices, consider these points:

- Perhaps your marketing material isn't doing a good job of conveying your worth. Look at your Web site, brochure, newsletter, business card, etc., with a critical eye. Do they express your experience, quality, and other characteristics in such a way as to justify your prices? Have a trusted friend, preferably someone who represents your target customer, review your marketing material. Or, hire a marketing or communications professional to assess how you and your company come across to potential customers.

- Re-evaluate your target customer. Maybe you're going after a smaller client when you should be targeting a higher-end client. For example, if you're a seasoned graphic designer who's worth the higher end of the pay scale, you might be better suited to corporate clients rather than small businesses.

- Reconsider your geographic target market. The going rate for products and services is generally higher in larger cities. A company located in a thriving metropolis is going to pay higher prices than a firm doing business in a smaller town off the beaten track.

- Modify your offerings to suit the market you're in. Let's say you're a product development consultant not having much luck selling your services to sole proprietors. Consider developing a group consulting rate where each person pays a lower rate, but together, the group meets or exceeds your fees for a one-hour session.

The most important step you can take to ensure you are running a successful business is to track your costs and profits every three months.

Let us repeat that: The most important step you can take to ensure you are running a successful business is to track your costs and profits every three months. Knowing, rather than just assuming, the financial reality of your business is critical to the health and well-being of your company because you must know for certain whether your prices are still covering your expenses and making you a profit. Don't just do it at tax time—you'll have lost your opportunity to adjust your strategy.

Bright Idea	Set a recurring task in your calendar to re-evaluate your pricing structure to be sure it's still working for you. Overhead expenses and variable expenses, such as the cost of materials, can change. Over time, you may also find ways to make your processes more efficient.

FILTERING THROUGH THE FEEDBACK

You've narrowed down your business idea, you know who your customers are and how much you're going to charge them. It's time to get other people's opinions. Ideally, you'd ask people who could potentially be your customers, but if that isn't possible, getting some feedback is better than none at all. You can ask your family and friends, but keep in mind they may not be completely honest with you because they want to be supportive regardless of their opinions or they don't want to hurt your feelings. A local business class or networking meeting would be a great place to introduce your idea. Plus, you'll have the added benefit of starting to build your network of contacts (more on that in our chapter on networking).

How to start the conversation

Start off by asking for permission: I'm considering starting my own business and would love to get your feedback. May I ask you a few questions?

- I'm thinking of opening a downtown doggie daycare center. Would you, or someone you know, have a need for that service?
- My hours would be Monday through Friday from 7 a.m. to 6 p.m. Would that suit your needs?
- I would charge $20 per visit. Does that seem reasonable to you?
- What questions or concerns do you have about this business?
- Have you ever used such a service before? If so, what did you like about it? What did you dislike about it?

- Do you know anyone who uses doggie day care; if so, could you put me in touch with him or her?

The most important question to ask during this conversation is "why?" If someone tells you he would never use your service, don't assume it's because he doesn't have a dog. Ask why. You may learn that although he does have a dog, he wouldn't trust his pooch to someone else. That doesn't mean no one would buy your service. But, it does mean you've uncovered an obstacle that you can address as you create your business and turn it into a selling point. (For example: We know you wouldn't trust your precious pet to just anyone. Our Web cams let you watch your pal throughout the day.)

How to use negative feedback to test an idea

If someone gives you negative feedback, your first reaction may be to ignore it. After all, you've already put a lot of effort into your business idea and you don't want to hear any criticism. But that's exactly what you need to hear at this point because you can use it to your advantage. We can hear what you're thinking: "Uncle Jimmy is an idiot." That may be true, but he may still provide you with a valuable opportunity to fine-tune your idea.

Let's say Uncle Jimmy's first reaction to your doggie daycare idea is, "Oh, yeah, right, like you're gonna want twenty big, slobbering dogs running around your house. That's the stupidest idea you've come up with yet." Thank Unc for his time and then give serious consideration to what he said. Here are some productive follow-up thoughts:
- Number of dogs: Gee, I never said I'd have twenty dogs. That would be too much. I figure I can handle ten with no problem. So I'll have a maximum limit of ten dogs per day.
- Size of dogs: Big dogs? I was picturing Yorkies and Chihuahuas, not Rottweilers and Bull Mastiffs. Wait a minute! What if I specialized and took in only dogs 20 pounds and under? Then, people wouldn't worry about their tiny dogs getting stepped on. Great marketing niche!
- Cleanliness factor: Slobber? Can't do much about that, except make sure I have plenty of paper towels. And to use a space that's easily cleaned.

Maybe Uncle Jimmy's delivery was annoying, but look at what resulted from his comments: you further refined your business idea. Good work!

Bright Idea	Host a wine-and-cheese focus group
	Invite potential customers, friends, and/or family to a wine-and-cheese party. Present your business idea and ask for feedback about your idea, target market, pricing, and whatever else you want opinions about. Consider assigning a facilitator who can keep the meeting on track and free you up to listen objectively. Your local Small Business Administration (SBA) office may offer this service or you could hire a business coach. Have someone else take notes for you, not only on comments, but also on participants' reactions. Because it can be difficult to run the session and catch everyone's body language, it may be worth videotaping the session so you can study reactions and comments later.

A QUICK WRAP-UP

You've tested your business idea and you now know this can happen after all. It's a little scary, isn't it? Your heart may be beating a little faster and you may even feel lightheaded. It's not that your pantyhose are too tight, it's that you've just stepped onto the Adventure Ride of Your Life. Take a deep breath, wave your hands in the air, and smile big. Enjoy the ride!

REFLECTIONS

What are three things you're taking away from this chapter?

1. _____
   _____
   _____

2. _____
   _____
   _____

3. _____
   _____
   _____

COACHING FOR SUCCESS

- What part of "me" is most important to bring to this business?

   _____
   _____
   _____
   _____

- What did I learn from the feedback I received from others? How did I handle the feedback?

   _____
   _____
   _____
   _____
   _____

- What is the next step for me to take to refine my idea?

   _____
   _____
   _____
   _____

TOOLKIT

Here are a few resources to help you determine the feasibility factor of your business.

Books

- *Do What You Love, The Money Will Follow: Discovering Your Right Livelihood*, by Dr. Marsha Sinetar, is an inspirational book that explores the importance and success of running a business you are passionate about.
- *Made to Stick: Why Some Ideas Survive and Others Die*, by Chip Heath and Dan Heath, is often funny and always eye-opening. This book describes the key principles that make some ideas so memorable.
- *Purple Cow: Transform Your Business by Being Remarkable*, by Seth Godin, explains how to develop a product or service that stands out from a crowd.

Articles

- "How Good Is Your Big Idea," by Tim Knox, an online article at www.nationalbusiness.org/nbaweb/Newsletter2006/2176.htm.
- "Is Your Business Idea Feasible," by Timothy Faley, an online article at: www.inc.com/resources/startup/articles/20051001/analysis.html.

Web sites

- AllBusiness.com is dedicated to growing business, with articles, videos, blogs, and more. This particular article helps you determine your target audience so you can decide if your business idea fits: www.allbusiness.com/marketing/segmentation-targeting/2588-1.html.
- Arkansas Small Business Development Center has many excellent downloadable guides and checklists, including a comprehensive feasibility workbook with a detailed pricing formula.
  Go to http://asbdc.ualr.edu/consulting/feasibility.pdf.
- Senior Core of Retired Executives (SCORE) provides free online tools, workshops, online business counseling, and lists of resources for entrepreneurs (www.score.org). There are more than 380 SCORE chapters throughout the United States that offer in-person business counseling and low-cost workshops; check out your local chapter to determine if it provides the services you need.

Appendix A

Overhead expenses

Use this list to identify expenses that contribute to your overhead rate. It's often easier to use a monthly projection.

EXPENSE	COST
Accountant/Bookkeeper	
Administrative Assistant	
Advertising	
Attorney fees	
Automobile: maintenance	
Automobile: gasoline	
Automobile: lease	
Books	
Collateral materials (e.g., brochures, business cards, letterhead, newsletters)	
Construction costs	
Dues (e.g., networking groups)	
Entertainment	
Equipment (e.g., computer, fax, phone, pager)	
Fees (e.g., trade show cost)	
Furniture	
Insurance: (e.g., automobile, life, disability, health)	
Licenses/permits	
Office supplies	
Postage	
Professional development	
Rent	
Salary	
Software	
Web site (design, hosting, etc.)	
Other	
TOTAL	

CHAPTER THREE

PLANNING YOUR BUSINESS

"Failing to plan is planning to fail."
—Effie Jones, teacher and champion for women leaders

In this chapter, you'll learn how to:
- Create an action plan.
- Find out what you don't know.
- Develop your business plan.
- Prepare for the unexpected.
- Design your exit strategy.

Planning provides the opportunity to think about the future when you're not knee deep in it. If you think of your first year in business as a journey, then this is your roadmap. You might change directions, and that's OK, but at least you'll be prepared for the trip. Even if you've jumped into your business without spending too much planning time, you might find it useful to step back for a moment and use the information and exercises in this chapter. Think of it as a rest stop to reset your compass.

Some of us enjoy planning more than others. For some, planning is the very reason to do something. For others, it's an end that justifies the means and the sooner it's over, the better. Let's face it, when you have a great idea and you're ready, willing, and able to make it happen, you don't want to get slowed down by having to plan, do you? Actually, you do. A little planning today makes for better results tomorrow. Just be sure not to get so caught up in the planning stage that you never put your ideas into action. (If you stick with us, we won't let that happen!) Whether you like to plan or not, remember that your new business is just that—a business. If you treat it like a hobby, then that's all it will ever be. Be a professional business owner and take the time to plan.

BEGIN AT THE END

Sounds kinda Zen, doesn't it? Luckily you don't have to be a yogi or a Tibetan monk to benefit from this idea. All you have to do is think about what you want the end result of your business to be. Once you know what your primary objective is, you can identify the steps you need to take to achieve it. By starting with the big idea—your objective—you make a huge, seemingly unattainable task more manageable by breaking it into smaller steps.

Let's say your main business objective is to become a successful real estate agent. From where you're sitting right now, this may seem like an impossible dream, but if we break it down into action steps, you'll see that it's not only in your power to achieve every step—you can do something about it today! Here's what a simple action plan might look like.

OBJECTIVE:
Make $100,000 in real estate commissions by the end of next year.

This year:
- Choose a realty company to join.
- Become known in my target community as the real estate agent of choice.
- Sell x number of houses (x being the number of houses needed to meet my objective).

This month:
- Meet with three realty companies.
- Attend four networking meetings (and be sure to read our networking chapter for great tips on this topic).
- Figure out how many homes I'll need to sell to make $100,000.

Today:
- Call three realty companies and schedule meetings for next week.
- Check out the Web sites for the state's Chamber of Commerce meetings and register for at least one event this month.

Exercise

Action plan

- Write your objective below.
- List the steps you have to take to achieve that objective, breaking them down by year, then month, and finally, what you can do today.

Objective:

_____

_____

_____

This year, I will:

- _____
- _____
- _____
- _____
- _____
- _____
- _____
- _____

This month, I will:

- _____
- _____
- _____
- _____
- _____
- _____

Today, I will:

- _____
- _____
- _____

KEEPING IT REAL

You've defined your goals for the year, the month, and today … good job! To be sure you stay focused, it may help to set up a system to track your progress. Here's the good news: there's a system for everyone.

You can get high-tech with electronic gadgets that offer automated reminders, choose a sophisticated paper planning system, or go the simple route of a pad and pen. Which is the best system? Whichever one you'll use consistently. Here are a few options to help you manage your time and your goals.

System	Pros	Cons
Computer-based system, such as Microsoft Outlook, which includes task management	• It's easy to update. • You can schedule reminders to pop up on the appointment day and time. • You can print out your tasks. • It has an integrated calendar and address book.	• You have to be on your computer to view or make changes to your goals or tasks. • Periodic upgrades are necessary. • It isn't portable (even a laptop is too bulky to carry around all the time).
A personal digital assistant (PDA), such as a Palm or Pocket PC	• It's easy to update. • It's portable—fits in your purse. • You can sync it to your computer. • You can schedule reminders that pop up on the appointed day and time.	• You could lose it (but if you keep it backed up on your computer at least you won't lose your data). • You have to learn how to write with a stylus. • It's one more device to carry around.
Paper planner, such as Day-Timer	• No technical knowledge is needed. • It's portable. • Systems include calendar, address book, and notepad.	• Updates can be time-consuming and require rewriting. • It's bulkier than a PDA. • It isn't easy to share information.

FIND OUT WHAT YOU DON'T KNOW

If you believe it's important to learn something new every day, then you're in for a treat as a business owner—there seems to be an endless stream of opportunities to learn from. This is usually great, occasionally not so good, and either way it's best to be proactive. Shorten your learning curve by discovering as much as you can about what it takes to run a business. There are a variety of organizations that offer seminars, courses, and online workshops to get you up to speed (some of which are mentioned in the Resources section at the end of this chapter). You can also pick up valuable information by:

• Subscribing to newsletters written by industry organizations.
• Talking to the people you meet at networking events.

- Auditing a college course.
- Reading magazines specific to your industry (if you don't know of any, ask the reference librarian at your local library).

Expect the unexpected—or at least plan for it. We hope that the winds of fortune bring you only goodness, but the fact is, yucky things happen to nice people. What you need to do right now, while you're in a place of comfort and safety, is to think about what you would do if you get sick; or if your office burns down, gets flooded, is shaken by an earthquake, or blown away by a hurricane; or if you lose a major client. Some of the best events in life can also throw your business into a tailspin. Think about how you would handle getting pregnant, having to relocate, or managing a major growth spurt in your business.

Is there a part of your business you can run "virtually" if you were home recovering from knee surgery? Who can you call to be your back-up? Financial planners say you should have three to six months' worth of money to live on in the event you are unable to work. Are you ready?

In Her Words

"Make sure you know what your insurance policy does—and doesn't—cover. We had a $2 million insurance policy, but found out too late that it only covered personal injury, not loss of equipment. We never expected that we would exceed that level of coverage."

—Shannon Mace, co-owner, ReMax American Dream
(www.WorkingForTheAmericanDream.com)

Tragically, Shannon speaks from experience. Her office was located in Bernat Mills, Uxbridge, Mass., which burned to the ground in 2007. Shortly after, Lori Adamo, president of Code Red Business Continuity Services (www.CodeRedbcs.com), wrote an article about disaster preparedness, using the Bernat Mills fire as a case study. Of disaster preparedness in general, Lori says that "it's not just about protecting your business information, communications, and technology, but the people and facilities as well." Hear our full interview with Lori and read her disaster preparedness article on our Web site.

When unplanned events strike, your entire life can be overwhelmed with emotion and reaction, even if that event is a happy one, such as having a baby. It will be a comfort to know your business plan already includes ways to handle these challenges so that, should you ever find yourself in one of these circumstances, you can refer to the plan you created when you weren't packing, bailing water out of your office, or in labor. The following exercise will guide you along.

Exercise

Contingency plan
Answer the following questions, then print these pages and keep them in a safe place.

If you have to relocate:
* How will you communicate your new address?

_____
_____
_____
_____

* What resources will you need to help you with the physical move?

_____
_____
_____

* How much time will you need? Is it a weekend project or will you have to notify clients that you'll be away during business hours?

_____
_____
_____

If you experience a major growth in your business:
* At what point will you need to hire contractors?

_____
_____
_____

* Will you refer business to other practitioners? (If so, consider a way to receive a referral fee.)

_____
_____
_____
_____

- Will you bring in a partner to divvy up responsibilities? If so, whom-might that be?

  _____

  _____

  _____

  _____

If you get pregnant (wow—a whole nine months to plan!):
- Which clients will you notify in advance that you won't be available during maternity leave?

  _____

  _____

  _____

- Which tasks or projects can you frontload?

  _____

  _____

  _____

  _____

  _____

- If you'll bring in an outside contractor for temporary assistance, whom will that be?

  _____

  _____

  _____

- If you hire a virtual assistant to handle calls and small projects, whom will you consider?

  _____

  _____

  _____

- Do you have, or should you consider, short-term disability insurance?

  _____

  _____

  _____

If you become too sick to work for a long period of time:
- How long can you be out of work until you need to make arrangements for someone else to step in?

  _____

  _____

  _____

  _____

- Whom can you rely on to provide services on your behalf for the interim?

  _____
  _____
  _____
  _____

- Do you have long-term disability insurance?

  _____
  _____
  _____

If you lose a major client:
- Who are your top-tier prospects that you can begin to cultivate when it becomes apparent this may happen?

  _____
  _____
  _____

- How will you increase your networking efforts?

  _____
  _____
  _____
  _____

- How can you increase business or offer additional services to existing clients?

  _____
  _____
  _____
  _____

- What expenses can you immediately reduce or eliminate so the loss doesn't cripple you?

  _____
  _____
  _____
  _____

If a natural disaster strikes:
- How will you secure your office equipment?

  _____
  _____
  _____
  _____

- Do you have computer file backups in a secure location?

- How will you communicate with your clients, staff, and vendors?

- What will you need to take with you? If you have to work from another location, what are the essentials?

CHART THE COURSE TO YOUR SUCCESS

Starting your own business is like going somewhere new: you have to know your destination and plan your route. Once you're familiar with the territory, you might decide to modify your directions. And when something changes—road construction or your destination—you make a few more changes.

A business plan is your roadmap, and it's critical to have no matter what kind of business you're starting. It's not something you need only if you're asking a bank for money. Creating your business plan is an excellent exercise in thinking through all the aspects of running your business. Some areas may not apply to you; no problem. You don't have to fill out every section (as long as you're not applying for a loan). But you have to at least give it some thought.

YOUR BUSINESS PLAN MIGHT INCLUDE THESE TOPICS:

- Business profile: Mission statement; description of your business, target market and customers; growth trends in this business.
- About you: Educational credentials, related work experience.
- Equipment: Computers, telephones, scanners, fax machine.
- Organization and insurance: Business entity, consultants needed (attorney, accountant, banker, etc.), licenses, insurance, zoning.
- Accounting and cash flow: Business records, tax issues, purchasing, inventory control.
- Financing: Cash sources, expenses.
- E-commerce: Strategy, budgeting, competition.
- Marketing: Strategy, advertising and promotions, competition.
- Growth: Expansion, problem resolution.

The more comprehensive your business plan, the better. But let's face it, the idea of creating a 14-page document can be daunting. If you're hesitant about writing a full business plan, use this exercise to start a plan you can build on.

Exercise — Back-of-the-napkin business plan

Write down your responses to the following questions for a simple business plan that is a very good start to the full-blown version.

What is your product or service?	
What do you want your company to be known for?	
How will your clients find you?	
What do you want people to say about you?	
How will this business create the life you want?	
How will you define success?	
How can you collaborate with other business people?	
Describe your ideal client.	
What challenges do you have to overcome?	
What's your exit strategy?	
How will you fund your start-up costs?	
What is your one-year revenue goal?	

GIVING YOUR NOTICE

How will you "quit" your business someday? *Wait a minute*, you're thinking. This book is all about starting my new business. What's this talk about ending it already? Fact is, there are as many reasons to end a business as there are to start one. Maybe you found another business to pursue. Perhaps you're ready to retire. Heck, maybe you're taking the millions you made from your business and are moving to Tahiti to work on your tan. What will you do with your business? What will happen to your clients? In other words, what's your exit strategy?

Now is the time to think about these things, so that when the time comes, you'll be ready. You don't have to do anything, just write it down somewhere. Here's how we three plan to get out of Dodge City when we decide to "retire" from our respective businesses:

The Sassy Ladies Say

Michelle: I am using my company, Precision Web Marketing, to create new, Web-based businesses (such as www.TheSassyLadies.com) to generate residual income to support my retirement. When Exit Day comes, I will sell my share in Precision (to employees, perhaps).

Wendy: When it's time to move away from Corley Hanson Associates, I will resign my position as president, have the business evaluated so I'll know the value of my stock, and decide if I want to sell all or some of my shares. I'll request to be hired as a contractor so I can continue doing the work I'm passionate about, but can have more time for other ventures.

Miriam: When I close my communication consulting business, I'll meet with writers I know who specialize in the same areas I do. Then I'll let all my business clients—past and present—know I'm closing up shop. I'll give them the names of writers whom they might be interested in working with.

A QUICK WRAP-UP

When you go on vacation, don't you choose your destination first and then plan how to get there, what to do once you're there, and how to get back home? Even a day of running errands goes smoother when you decide where you're going before you leave the house. Give the same attention to how you'll run your business and you'll have more time and energy to enjoy it.

REFLECTIONS

What are three things you're taking away from this chapter?

1. _____
   _____
   _____

2. _____
   _____
   _____

3. _____
   _____
   _____

COACHING FOR SUCCESS

- Which of the following (or other) areas will I either need to develop my skills in or hire others to do?
  - Finance
  - Accounting
  - Marketing
  - Web site development
  - Product design and production

- What is my personal learning plan for the coming year?

  _____
  _____
  _____
  _____

- How will I track my goals and my success? (This is a great question to ask other business owners to get ideas that may work for you.)

  _____
  _____
  _____
  _____

TOOLKIT

Take advantage of these resources to help your planning efforts.

Books

- *New Venture Creation: Entrepreneurship for the 21st Century* with PowerWeb and New Business Mentor CD, by Jeffry A. Timmons and Stephen Spinelli; specifically, Chapter 11, which has questions, exercises, and in-depth business plan samples.
- *Anatomy of a Business Plan: A Step-by-Step Guide to Building a Business and Securing Your Company's Future,* by Linda Pinson, offers sample business plans and worksheets and tips galore.
- *The 7 Habits of Highly Effective People,* by Dr. Stephen R. Covey, has a strong following of people who used this comprehensive book to take control of their professional and personal lives through effective time management, productivity principles, and a general attitude readjustment.
- *The E-Myth Revisited: Why Most Small Businesses Don't Work and What to Do About It,* by Michael E. Gerber, explains how to balance business priorities to maximize success and clarifies the difference between working "on" your business and "in" your business.

Products

Remote PC access—Access your computer files from any computer via the Internet using software available.

- www.GoToMyPC.com

Online backup systems—These Web-based systems automatically backup your document, photo, and Outlook files and make it easy to restore lost data.

- http://mozy.com
- https://www.titanize.com

Web sites

Explore all these Web sites have to offer, and especially the sections we've noted that pertain specifically to planning.

- *Entrepreneur Magazine's* business start-up kits: These comprehensive, step-by-step guides provide detailed info on evaluating and financing franchise businesses. Some libraries and Small Business Development Center offices may carry these and allow you to review them in the office. www.smallbizbooks.com/cgi-bin/

SmallBizBooks/index.html?cam=Ecom&cid=Footer&size=TL
- Maine Small Business Development Centers' "Starting Your Small Business" online program is free. It focuses on planning, marketing, and more. www.MaineSbdc.org/train_login.cfm
- SCORE: You'll find an excellent template for a business plan, as well as other documents, at www.score.org/template_gallery.html.
- U.S. Small Business Administration:
  ○ Developing a Business Plan—Go to www.sba.gov/training/courses.html and click on "Free Online Courses" on the right side of the page.
  ○ Report of demographics specific to women-owned businesses: www.sba.gov/advo/research/rs280tot.pdf

Other sites worth browsing as you plan:
- Center for Women & Enterprise: www.cweonline.org
- Inc.: www.inc.com
- Entrepreneur: www.entrepreneur.com
- National Association of Women Business Owners: www.nawbo.com
- National Federation of Independent Business: www.nfib.com
- United States Chamber of Commerce: www.uschamber.com/sb/default
- The United States Small Business Administration: www.sba.gov
- Women's Business Enterprise National Council: www.wbenc.org
- WomenEntrepreneur.com: www.womenentrepreneur.com

THE SASSY LADIES' WEB SITE RESOURCES

Here's an additional resource, free of charge, on our Web site at www.TheSassyLadies.com/StartupChapter3. And don't forget to post questions you have about planning on our blog to find out how others have successfully handled a particular challenge.
- Action Plan
  An action planning tool to help you identify steps you need to take to accomplish your goals.

CHAPTER FOUR

WORKING FROM YOUR HOME OFFICE

"Those who make the worst use of their time are the first to complain of its shortness."
—Jean de la Bruyère (1645–1696), French essayist

In this chapter, you'll learn how to:
- Set up an efficient home office.
- Manage your time wisely.
- Decide when it's time to get help.
- Choose the best systems and technologies to keep you organized.

Setting up your home office is actually more of a process than it is a task. What works for you when you first start your business may not work six months down the road. This chapter will give you strategies and resources you can use to keep your home base working for you. If your first year of business is a journey, setting up your home office is like packing for the trip. When you go camping, you don't leave home without the camp stove, tent, flashlights, bug spray, and marshmallows; when you get to your destination, you have the necessities and can relax and focus on the fun part. When you're embarking on your business adventure, the gear changes, but not the idea: get yourself in order and you will be more relaxed and productive. Even if you've had a home office for some time, this chapter will help you fine-tune the setup and systems you have.

Your home office might be a spare room, a corner of the basement, a closet, or a desk. At this point, it might even be a temporary space on the kitchen counter. No matter how grand or humble the space you've staked out as your home office is, you have to set it up so that it works for you. Whether you plan to spend most of your time away from it or it's where you'll spend most of your waking hours, you need to create a space that lets you be as productive as possible.

Right from the start, get used to thinking of this space as your office. Refer to it that way when you're talking to clients, as in, "I'll check on that as soon as I get back to my office." You are a businesswoman running your own company, even if it is a one-woman show. Treat this new venture seriously in all aspects. This doesn't mean you can't have fun with it or that you have to take yourself too seriously. It means that when people perceive your confidence in your business, they'll have confidence in you.

TOOLS OF YOUR TRADE

What you need in your home office will largely depend on your business. The basics usually include:

- **Telephone line**. This could be your cell phone, your home phone, or a dedicated line. If it's doing double duty for personal and business use, be sure your voice mail greeting is professional. No kids, karaoke, or dogs barking to the tune of "We Will Rock You." Create a simple, generic message that won't confuse people whether they're calling for you or your 17-year-old son. A simple, all-purpose message: "Sorry to have missed your call. Please leave a message with the best time to reach you. Thank you."

- **E-mail address**. When you first start out, it's acceptable to have a free e-mail account with the cable company or Web service such as Gmail. Eventually, though, you should secure a business-oriented domain name, even if you don't have a Web site yet, so you can have a more professional e-mail address.

- **Post office box**. You can certainly have your business mail sent to your home, but you might not want to have your home address be so public. A small post office box is well worth the investment to project a professional image and protect your privacy.

- **Printer**. If you print mostly text documents, an inkjet printer may be fine. When you need high-quality laser printouts on occasion, you can use print-on-demand services from an office supply store such as Staples or Office Max. You'll pay a per-sheet price, can send the files via e-mail, and pick up the printouts in the store nearest you.

- **Fax machine**. You can get a decent printer/scanner/fax combo for less than $200. Or, if you don't send a lot of faxes and you have a scanner, you can scan documents and use an on-demand fax service such as www.efax.com, which charges a monthly rate (less than $20 per month) for a set number of pages per month. Either way, it's one less errand to run.

SETTING UP YOUR SPACE

Clear your office space of anything that isn't related to your business. Pretend for a moment that your workspace is located in a corporate office—would it fit in? Of course it's appropriate to personalize your space with photos of your kids or your well-earned Mardi Gras beads, but find another place for the spare box of light bulbs and the sweater you keep meaning to hand wash. (And ... hello? Hand wash? Please.)

Organize your space so everything you need on a daily basis is within easy reach and it's no trouble keeping your work area neat. If you're constantly battling piles, knocking over your pen cup, and your stapler hasn't had staples in it since the Republicans controlled the Senate, it's time for a few changes.

- Your phone, printer, and other frequently used items should be within arm's length when you're sitting at your desk.
- Keep only the things you use every day on top of your desk. Store everything else in drawers and filing cabinets.
- Stackable trays keep documents sorted. Label them for easy reference. Consider categories such as: Reading, Action Required, To Be Filed.
- Turn a spare closet into dedicated office storage to keep office supplies and materials you need but don't use every day.
- Make the most of your wall space by hanging a few sturdy shelves for reference books, project binders, etc.
- Hang a bulletin board for reminders, a calendar, and small notes that would otherwise clutter your desk or get lost.

Here's the ideal home office setup for each of us:

The Sassy Ladies Say

Michelle: My home office is a built-in corner desk in our finished basement. What I love about it is that it has lots of shelves and cabinets—over the desk, under the desk, behind the desk. There's a place for everything. I also bought a set of pretty baskets that provide decorative desktop storage for colored pencils, paper clips, Post-it notes, file folders, etc.

Wendy: A few years ago, I splurged and had California Closets build my office: desk, shelves, and filing cabinets.

Miriam: I converted a spare room into an office. I keep my supplies in the closet. A filing cabinet holds my active and recent project files. My reference books are tucked into a bookcase. The only files I keep on my desk are what I'm working on today. And on the wall, I framed quotes that inspire me, including the lyrics to "I Hope You Dance."

OFFICE AWAY FROM OFFICE

Home may be where the heart is, but it's not always where your mind is. Husbands, partners, kids, dogs, cats, and noisy neighbors may be too much of a distraction. Not to mention the laundry, dust bunnies, and the hundred chores that will take just five minutes to do. Nothing takes five minutes. Except for spending $50 at Target, but that's another issue.

One option is to pack up your laptop and head to your "satellite" office, which could be anywhere you can focus on your work. If you need wireless access, there are plenty of establishments that welcome laptoppers with free Wi-Fi access—Panera Bread and Fresh City are two well-known chains. Don't forget to buy a snack; it's a fair trade for renting space! Many libraries also have wireless access. And while you can't get a tall, iced mocha drink there, it is quiet and comfortable.

Ideally, you will find a way to work at your home office when you need to; that is, after all, one of the perks of working for yourself. Nothing says, "I'm the boss" like negotiating a new contract in your fuzzy slippers. You might have to schedule your phone time in the morning when the kids are in school or plan on writing your proposals in the afternoon when things are quiet.

MANAGING YOUR TIME

The right combination of time management strategies is different for everyone. Like finding just the right party dress, you may have to try a few things out to find what works best for you. One thing is for certain: Making the most of your time means more than trying to figure out how little sleep you can survive on. Here are 11 reasonable ways to manage your time:

- Begin each week with a list of the most important things that must get done, followed by those things that should get done. Revisit this list first thing each morning to be sure you're on track. This way, you won't waste time focusing on tasks that really could wait.
- Go to work the same time each day so you can establish routines to keep you on track.
- Schedule time to get work done, not just meeting time. It's unrealistic to think you can have five meetings, create a presentation for next week's meeting with your new client, and keep up with your e-mail correspondence in 8 or 10 hours. Protect this valuable chunk of time by not answering the phone or e-mail; focus on the task at hand.

- Work with your internal clock. If you are a morning person, that's when you should schedule your toughest tasks.
- Leave time in each day's schedule for emergencies and unplanned activities.
- Make time for down time. Although this sounds like the opposite of being productive, it's actually an effective way to reboot your brain. Take the dog for a walk, sip a cup of tea while doing a crossword puzzle, or read a poem. Taking a few minutes to shift your focus can actually help you refocus on the task at hand with better clarity.
- A place for everything and everything in its place. If you take the time to put things away in their proper place, you'll save a bundle of time. We know, Mom used to say the same thing. She wasn't wrong about everything.
- Stick to your expertise. For example, if you don't have the design skills, don't bother trying to create your own newsletter. The learning curve to create a professional-looking piece is too high. Hand it over to an expert.
- Confirm the deadline. Believe it or not, not all clients need everything tomorrow, but if you offer, they'll take you up on it. Find out what's driving the due date so you can plan a reasonable schedule.
- If you have the flexibility to run personal errands during weekdays, you'll spend less time on the weekends in traffic and in line at the dry cleaner, pharmacy, grocery store, etc. Make up your work time during the weekends if necessary. Welcome to flextime, be-your-own-boss style.
- If you feel you're working around the clock and still not getting everything done, record your activities for one week. List every 15-minute increment—include phone calls, meetings, e-mail correspondence, personal errands, etc. You'll be able to see how you're spending your time and whether there are opportunities to streamline or eliminate unnecessary time wasters. We've developed an easy tool for just this purpose—and it's free to you! See the link in the Web Site Resources section at the end of this chapter.

In Her Words

"The biggest myth about owning your own business is that you have to work around the clock. The truth is your business will be what you set it up to be."

—Joelle Jay, Pillar Consulting (www.pillar-consulting.com)

TECHNOLOGY TO THE RESCUE

Technology can be an amazing timesaver, if used wisely. Or, it can be a burden. The key is to choose the technology that works for you, not against you. Don't be afraid to try new technology, but if it's not working, ditch it. Here's a look at the pros and cons of a few of the most popular gadgets.

Gadget	How it works	Pro	Con
Personal digital assistant (PDA), such as a Palm or Pocket PC	This handheld electronic organizer stores your calendar, address book, notes, and more. Some have wireless Internet access.	It's easy to update. It fits in your purse. You can sync it to your computer. You can schedule automatic reminders.	You could lose it (but if you keep it backed up at least you won't lose your data). You have to write with a stylus.
Blackberry or iPhone	Similar to a PDA, these devices can be used to send and receive e-mail by connecting to available wireless networks; you can also access Web sites.	You have e-mail access no matter where you are.	You have e-mail access no matter where you are, which is also a con because it can be such a distraction.
Business card scanner	This gadget scans business cards into a digital address book.	Good if you need to keep track of hundreds of business contacts.	Not efficient if you don't continuously have a large number of new contacts.
Digital recorder	Because it records audio in digital format, you can upload recordings to your computer to store or send via e-mail.	Compact; great for recording notes on the run.	These messages must be downloaded to your PC before they can be sent.
Skype www.skype.com	Lets you use your computer to make and receive telephone calls via the Internet.	Provides conference calling, instant messaging, and file sharing. Phone calls to other Skype users are free. Paid version lets you accept phone calls from traditional phone users.	The other party must also have downloaded software and set up an account, which means you must plan in advance. Limited number of people can participate in group calls.

Basecamp http://basecamphq. com	Web-based project management system that provides a central location for files, whiteboards, milestones, e-mail, and more.	Everyone on your project can get to the same information, regardless of location or computer system.	As with any system, it's only effective as long as you keep it updated.

GOOD HABITS TO HAVE

Setting up and maintaining your home office isn't just about choosing the right tools; it's also about setting up the processes to keep you running smoothly. This is where a little preparation can save you lots of time and frustration later.

- **Backup your computer files**—Schedule this task every week. If you think this chore is a pain, imagine what it will be like to lose all your work and have to start over again or explain to a client why you've lost her information. Backing up your data could be as simple as copying your files onto a CD-ROM or an external hard drive. Just remember to keep the CD or drive in a different physical location than your computer because you're not just protecting your data in case your computer crashes. In the event of a fire, flood, or other disaster, it won't do you much good if your backup files are sitting two feet away from the computer that just got destroyed. You could also opt to use an online backup system, which will automatically backup your files (see the Toolkit section at the end of this chapter for a couple of options).

- **Review your invoices**—Set aside the same time each month to send out invoices and reminders for overdue balances.

- **Send out thank-you notes**—If someone sent you a lead that turned into business, send a note to express your appreciation. An e-mail is acceptable, but a handwritten card is even more impressive. And if you land a major client because of a referral, a small gift—such as chocolate or a plant—is appropriate. (See the Web site resources section at the end for an online card service that lets you select and mail cards from your computer.)

- **Manage your marketing**—In addition to providing excellent service, the most important thing you can do is stay on your target market's mind. Stick to your marketing plan (you do have one, don't you? If not, see the next chapter on that very subject) and distribute your newsletter, postcards, etc., on a regular basis.

- **Track your time each day**—If yours is a service business, keeping track of your time is critical so you know what your billable hours are. If you're charging by the project, this is also a good way to see if you're putting more hours in than you estimated. You'll find a link to our time tracker in the Web site resources section at the end of this chapter.
- **End each day by cleaning up the clutter from the day's work.** Make a to-do list for the next day. Be realistic—force yourself to prioritize so you can make the best use of your time.

In Her Words

"Everyone thinks that to be organized is to be neat. But even the neatest people are often disorganized. They might have ten neat piles reaching to the ceiling, but that doesn't mean they could find what they need in those piles. Someone not so neat may be able to find what he or she needs in a flash! My definition of being organized is: You can find what you need when you need it and you get everything done when it's due—without stress."

—Maria Gracia, founder, Get Organized Now! ™
(www.GetOrganizedNow.com)

GET ORGANIZED

Some of us would consider a root canal—without Novocain—less painful than approaching the topic of getting organized. It's the Holy Grail of life: finding the right combination of tools and tricks that will keep us from sobbing into our sleeves (because we can't remember to buy Kleenex) because we can't find a business card, missed an appointment, and forgot to follow-up with an important prospective client. Some of us need an entire book devoted to the topic of getting organized (see the Toolkit at the end of this chapter for a few titles), so we can only scratch the surface here, but it might be enough to keep you from losing your mind, unless you left it next to that business card and then we can't help you.

- Create a binder for every major project. Include a pocket folder in the front for open issues that have to be resolved; once they are, file them in the binder or discard.
- Keep a slim notebook inside each project file or binder. That's where you take notes for that project.
- Use index cards to write to-do items. This way, everything you have to do can be kept in one place, or sorted into appropriate folders:

calls to make, stuff to buy, tasks, etc.

- If you have Microsoft Office, get to know the powerful task list features. You can use colored flags, automatic reminders, and categories to organize your task list.
- If it takes you more than five minutes to find something, you need a new system.

Exercise **To-do list**

Despite your best intentions, you can only do so much in a day. And, everything can't be the highest priority. Be realistic and you set yourself up for success. Use this list to do just that.

A	HIGHEST PRIORITY – MUST GET DONE TODAY
	_____
	_____
	_____
	_____
	_____

B	SECOND PRIORITY – SHOULD GET DONE TODAY
	_____
	_____
	_____
	_____
	_____

C	THIRD PRIORITY – COULD GET DONE TODAY
	_____
	_____
	_____
	_____
	_____

Calling in the cavalry

You don't get extra points for trying to do everything yourself if you're running yourself into the ground. If you think you can't afford to outsource, figure out how much money you're losing by not spending your time doing what makes you the most money. Some experts to consider:

- **Accountant or bookkeeper**—One of the first people to hire to help you do the right thing at tax time.

- **Business coach**—When you need guidance, motivation, or someone to keep you focused, a business coach will provide the support you need to flourish.
- **Copywriter**—If you find your marketing materials aren't getting done because you don't know what to say or can't say it professionally, a business writer can help.
- **Designer**—Especially important for designing your logo and can also help with your Web site, newsletter, brochure, and business card design. Remember that you get what you pay for, so if you're using a free canned template, it's going to show.
- **Errand runner or personal concierge**—From delivering your work to clients to picking up your dry cleaning, an errand runner can save you oodles of time.
- **Marketer**—It pays to have an expert in this field to help you identify and reach your customers.
- **Personal assistant**—Sending out print materials, fielding phone calls, scheduling appointments and jobs, filing, bookkeeping, research, project management, recordkeeping … the list of how a personal assistant can help you is truly endless.
- **Technology guru**—If the thought of the "blue screen of death" appearing on your computer screen seconds before you finish your big document sends you into a panic, find yourself a reliable tech advisor.
- **Virtual assistant**—Does almost everything a personal assistant can do, remotely. And unlike a permanent assistant, you can call on this person only when you need a helping hand, so you're not paying someone when you don't really need his or her services.
- **Web manager**—An outdated Web site is worse than no Web site at all. If you can't make at least monthly updates, a Web manager can keep your site up to date.

Bright Idea Offer to barter your services for someone else's when you don't have the budget to pay outright. Sign an agreement that outlines what's being traded so that everyone's expectations and responsibilities are clear.

THE PLACE WHERE YOU LIVE—AND WORK

Cities and towns have regulations about what kind of business you can conduct in your home. For example, some towns prohibit a business that involves customer traffic in and out of your home. Start with your state's Web site to find out what the zoning laws are and what licenses you may be required to obtain.

A QUICK WRAP-UP

Don't feel that setting up your home office is an all or nothing endeavor. You can incorporate one thing at a time. Remember that simple is almost always better. Don't over-engineer your organization system or you'll spend more time staying organized than running your business. Above all, make your home office a place that inspires and energizes you. It's amazing what a clean desk, a few funky filing folders, and your favorite photo in a pretty frame can do.

REFLECTIONS

What are three things you're taking away from this chapter?

1. _____
   _____
   _____

2. _____
   _____
   _____

3. _____
   _____
   _____

COACHING FOR SUCCESS

- Sit in your office space and look around. How do you feel as you view your working space?

   _____
   _____
   _____

What three things could you do to minimize distractions to be more focused while you're working in your home office?

1. _____
   _____
   _____

2. _____
   _____
   _____

3. _____
   _____
   _____

What three things could you do to make your office more productive?

1. _____
   _____
   _____

2. _____
   _____
   _____

3. _____
   _____
   _____

TOOLKIT

Here are a few resources to help you set up your home office.

Books

- *Getting Things Done: The Art of Stress-free Productivity* by David Allen. We like this book because it acknowledges there are many types of organizational systems (paper, electronic, etc.), and gives you a framework to stay focused in whichever format you prefer.
- *Sabbath: Finding Rest, Renewal, and Delight in Our Busy Lives* by Wayne Miller. A collection of poems, stories, and ideas on how to create quiet, reflective spaces in our lives so we can be highly productive, but not stressed, all the other times.

Magazines

- *Real Simple*—The ultimate source for ways to, as the name says, make your life (including your home office) less complicated. Each month's issue is packed with organization tips, product reviews, even creative uses for ordinary household items.

Articles

- "Ten Ways to Organize and Simplify Bill Paying" by Maria Gracia, www.getorganizednow.com/ezbill.html
- "Ten Ways to Conquer Your Reading Pile" by Maria Gracia, www.getorganizednow.com/art-reading.html

Web sites

- David Allen is the productivity guru who created the Getting Things Done (GTD) system; his Web site is www.davidco.com.
- Get Organized Now! is Maria Gracia's site (www.GetOrganizedNow.com). Go there for a free Get Organized Now!™ Idea-Pak filled with tips and ideas to help you organize your home, your office, and your life. Plus, the site is packed with articles and checklists. Her book, *Finally Organized, Finally Free*, is organized by the place you need to organize (e.g., your desk, your kids' rooms).
- Kelly Forrister teaches the Getting Things Done system through seminars and individual coaching. Read her blog for tips and motivation at www.DavidCo.com/blogs/kelly/.
- OrganizingLA blog site has articles and tips on how to organize your space, including before-and-after pictures: http://www.organizingla.com/organizingla_blog/2007/02/post.html.

Products

- **Online backup systems**—These Web-based systems automatically backup your document, photo, and Outlook files and make it easy to restore lost data.
  - http://mozy.com
  - https://www.titanize.com
- **Project management**—Whether you're collaborating on projects with others or you'd just like to have one place to put files, tasks, notes, timelines, and other project-related material, a Web-based system gives you access from anywhere. Check out Basecamp at www.basecamphq.com, which we like because it has all the right features and is as easy to use as the company says it is.
- **Send Out Cards**—No more going to the store to buy cards, then having to run another errand to mail them. This online service makes it easy to stay in touch with your customers on a regular basis. You can even set reminders so no one gets forgotten. Check out www.SendOutCards.com/TheSassyLadies.

THE SASSY LADIES' WEB SITE RESOURCES

We're providing you access to an additional resource, free of charge, on our Web site at www.TheSassyLadies.com/StartupChapter4.

- Time Tracker
  Use this simple chart to track your hours for client billing or productivity and profit analysis.

We're always trying new products and services to stay organized, so check our blog often for ideas to keep you running smoothly—and at top speed.

CHAPTER FIVE

MARKETING YOUR BUSINESS

"Would you tell me please which way I ought to go from here?"
"That depends a good deal on where you want to get to," said the cat.
"I don't care much where," said Alice.
"Then it doesn't matter much which way you go," said the cat.
—*Alice's Adventures in Wonderland* by Lewis Carroll

In this chapter, you'll learn how to:
- Develop your brand.
- Decide which marketing strategies are best for you.
- Design a marketing plan to meet your sales goals.
- Get creative to get attention.

While marketing seems like the logical step after you complete the bulk of your planning and what you need to do just before you begin selling, it might not happen just that way. Life rarely follows a logical, linear sequence and neither does business. The good news is you can use the information in this chapter from the beginning of your marketing efforts or somewhere in the middle. If we continue with the metaphor that your first year in business is a journey, then this chapter helps put you on the map.

Marketing means many things to many people. For some, it's a creative and fun endeavor that is all about color, design, image, and language. For others, it is a process that uses a strategic series of promotional activities that attract the attention of potential customers and convinces them to buy. Both are right. In essence, marketing is how you communicate the value of your business to your target audience, and it takes a combination of creativity and logic to be successful.

THE NAME GAME
The first step in building your brand is coming up with your company's name. Perhaps nothing has kept entrepreneurs up at night more than this topic. There are companies that can help you create the right name for your business and they can be worth every penny. But it's important to keep in mind that a company name is not the ticket to success; it's

just one part of a marketing strategy. You can find the perfect company name and still not be successful. On the other hand, who would have thought these company names would be so successful?

- **The Christmas Tree Shop**—This store sells a lot more than just Christmas trees.
- **Kinko's**—Admit it; when these stores first started appearing, you didn't go in with your kids because you were afraid it was rated X.
- **Dell**—What does that have to do with computers?
- **Staples**—Pantry staples, just staples, what?

All of these brands are household names (at least in their market or region), which proves one thing: your name is not nearly as important as making sure you have a strong and clear focus on your product and its value to your customers.

That being said, how do you create the perfect name for your company?

- You could use part or all of your name. Sassy Lady Miriam simply uses her full name. Sassy Lady Wendy's business goes by Corley Hanson Associates, Inc., which combines her husband's and her last names. Keep in mind that, without a tagline (the slogan that appears with your company name), using just your name isn't descriptive, so people won't know right away what it is you do. Add a tagline to help people understand what you do; for example: Miriam Perry—Effective Communications. Or, Corley Hanson Associates—Making Your Business a Team Sport. Using just your name gives you flexibility should you decide to shift your business focus because you won't have to re-brand your company.
- Think about a characteristic that describes your company, such as speed, accuracy, service, innovation, etc. Play with synonyms for those words. Sassy Lady Michelle's company is Precision Web Marketing, which conveys the accuracy with which she serves her clients. On the plus side, using such a descriptive company name ensures people will get an immediate sense of what your company sells. However, it does keep you tied to a specific product or service.
- Choose a word that evokes the "tone" of your business. It's no coincidence that so many spa names sound so relaxing—Indulge, Revive, Bliss.
- Invent a word. Take the first half of one word and the last half of another to form a new word (FabuLess = fabulous and less),

combine two words (BlueWater), or just make one up completely (Fleeper's).

Bright Idea	**Host a naming party**
	Invite four to twelve people to a naming party. Begin by describing your business and answering any questions people have about your product or service. For twenty minutes, each person writes a word or phrase on an index card while you post them on a wall or board. To keep creative juices flowing, throw out word categories that participants can associate with your business (e.g., colors, animals, verbs, adjectives, food). After everyone goes home, choose your top twenty names, then whittle that down to your top ten, and from there, select your final.
Hear our brand development story about how we got our name, The Sassy Ladies, on our Web site blog.

You'll probably end up with a few names. Keep narrowing the list down to three or four. This is a good time to check with your Secretary of State's office to be sure the name isn't already in use. If it is, that doesn't necessarily mean you can't use it, but you wouldn't want to be confused with another company. You'll have to file with the Secretary of State, which amounts to letting them know whom you're doing business as so they know whom to tax. If you decide to protect your company name to prevent other companies from using the same name, consider getting it trademarked, which you can hire an attorney to do or do it yourself through the United States Patent and Trademark Office.

Once you have a name you think will work, run it by half a dozen people. More times than not, you'll have to provide some context for your name, but it shouldn't require a whole lot of explanation. You can say, "My company name is Fleeper; I sell fleece sleeping bags for dogs." You shouldn't have to explain that the name Fleeper is "fleece" and "sleeper" put together. Some people will love your company name. Others may wrinkle their nose or look confused. Resist the urge to be defensive; accept their feedback gracefully.

Here are a few issues to consider about the responses you might get:

- **It doesn't describe what your product (or service) is**. It doesn't have to. What does the name Kraft tell you about the company? Nothing. Which is why the company writes "Kraft Foods" as a tagline—to give you context for what it sells.
- **Your company name isn't catchy**. It doesn't have to be. Your tagline might be catchy, but what's really important is how well you

connect what you're selling to your customers' needs. The name McDonald's isn't catchy, but it's pretty successful.

- **It's hard to pronounce or spell**. That's worth a second thought. Your company name should be easy to say because you want people talking about how great your product is, not how much of a tongue twister your business name is.
- **It's too cutesy (or serious or ...)**. If you're a financial advisor and someone tells you your company name, Fanny's Figures, is cutesy, you'll want to think about whether that's the image you want to convey. If you're running a doll shop, maybe cutesy is the right image.

All feedback is valuable; however, if you really feel strongly that you have a name that suits your business, don't be afraid to go with it despite negative feedback from a few people. Not everyone loved The Sassy Ladies when we solicited feedback during our naming process, but the majority of people did react positively and we felt it was the right name, so we went with it. Since then, we have attracted attention based solely on our name because we stand out from the pack. We've received so much positive feedback about our name that we know, without a doubt, we made the right decision.

A WORD ABOUT WEB SITE NAMES

It's getting harder to name companies because it's important that your Web site URL include your company's name, and a lot of domain names are taken. It's why companies are starting to invent words. You can also get creative by adding a word before or after your company name for your domain name. For example, a wine merchant whose company name is The Wine Store, may have to get the Web site domain name TheOnlineWineStore.com.

To check if the domain name you want is available, go to a Web site hosting service, such as www.GoDaddy.com or www. NetworkingSolutions.com, where you can search for a domain name.

TAG, YOU'RE IT!

A tagline is the phrase that comes after the brand name and reinforces the company's brand. For example:
- Pampered Chef: Discover the chef in you
- BMW: Sheer driving pleasure
- The Sassy Ladies: Wisdom for the spirited entrepreneur

You don't have to have a tagline, but it does help your customer remember your product or service. Developing a strong tagline means identifying the essence of your product or services. Even if you're not going to publish a tagline as part of your logo, it's worth coming up with a tagline to use when you describe your company to people.

LOGO LOGIC

Your logo is the visual component of your brand. There are two types of logos:

- **Text**—The name of the company in a distinctive typeface, called a treatment. Below are two examples: one of The Sassy Ladies' logo and one of Wendy's coaching company. Each treatment includes the typeface, color, and the way the letters are shaped. The logos look the same whether they appear in print, online, or on a T-shirt.

- **Graphical**—A picture or graphic is added to the company name. Logo graphics should always strongly support the brand. To the right is Michelle's company logo. In addition to a specific typeface treatment, a graphic of an arrow hitting a bull's-eye reinforces the message that her company provides targeted solutions.

No matter which logo style you choose, it must look crisp and professional. This is not where you try to save money by creating your own logo; homemade logos almost always look amateurish, which is exactly how you don't want your customers perceiving you or your company. Get referrals from other business owners for professional designers who specialize in logo development. Ask the designer for samples of his or her work; you're looking for logos that are professional and eye-catching. Request at least three proposals that include references. Be prepared for a wide range of prices; there are no standards in this industry. If a designer whose work you really like comes in with a price that's way out of your budget range, let her know you admire her work, but her proposal is too pricey. Let her know your budget and ask her what she can do for that amount; there's almost always room for negotiation.

BUILDING YOUR BRAND

Disney. Nike. McDonald's. Coach. It's not luck that each of these brand names evokes such a strong and distinct image, feel, or mood that we don't even have to describe their product lines for you to instantly recognize them. You just know. That's caché, baby. And that's what happens when you focus your resources to ensure there is no doubt in your customer's mind who you are and what you do. No one goes into a McDonald's restaurant and wonders where filet mignon is on the menu. No one searches the newspaper for a Coach coupon. Sure, these companies have deep pockets to spend on marketing, but that's not the only reason they're so well known. These companies also ensure their brands are well protected.

You can make sure you do the same thing by using your brand consistently and professionally. Your brand image, which is the way your company name, logo, and tagline are used together, should be used consistently, meaning:

- The colors are always the same. You don't change the typeface, which is blue, to red at Christmas.
- The typeface is consistent. You don't change the typeface just because you're tired of it.
- The logo is used on all official company material.

The idea behind building your brand is to build recognition. When your customers just glance at a postcard or Web site, you want them to immediately recognize your logo. When you use your logo in advertisements or if it appears on someone else's material because you've partnered with them or sponsored a program, be sure you have the chance to review your logo so you can confirm it is crisp and readable.

YOUR MARKETING PLAN

A basic marketing concept called "the four P's of marketing" provides a framework for developing your marketing plan:

- **Product**—what are you selling?
- **Price**—how much will you charge?
- **Place**—where will you provide this service?
- **Promotion**—how will you spread the word?

Most business owners can quickly rattle off the details of their product, price, and place, but falter when it comes to the promotion strategy. There are a number of ways to promote your business. Individually, they're known as *marketing tactics*. The ones you choose become your *marketing mix*. They include a Web site; collateral material, such as brochures and business cards; advertising; and networking. How you decide the right *marketing mix* for your promotional strategy will depend on four components, which are described in detail below: Your revenue goal; the number of customers you have to *reach* to meet that goal, commonly called reach; the frequency with which you need to get in front of your customers; and budget.

- **Revenue goal** – As Cheshire Cat points out in this chapter's opening quote, it doesn't matter which way you go if you don't know where you want to get to. You have to know what end result you want to have. How much revenue do you want to have in your first year? How many customers or orders will you need to achieve that goal? Once you know these answers, the marketing plan can begin to take shape.

Exercise

Determining your revenue goal

Determine the number of orders you must have to reach your revenue goal using the following formula: Your *revenue goal*, divided by your *average sale amount* equals the target number of customer orders.

Example: I would like to make $60,000 in sales in my first year. On average, my customers spend $500 per order, so I will need 120 customer orders.

Your target: I would like to make $ _____ in sales my first year. My average customer spends $ _____ per order, so I will need _____ customer orders to meet my goal.

Now that you know your goal, do you see that you need to sell a lot of products at a low cost to achieve your sales goals, or only a few high-cost items? This will make a difference once you start making decisions about the next three items.

- **Reach** – Let's say you figured out in the revenue exercise that you need 120 customer orders. How many customers must you convince to buy your product? Some customers will purchase more than once, but probably not more than 10%, so figure you'll you need about 108 customers. However, not all of the people you reach will buy. If you assume 5% of the audience become customers, then you have to reach out to 2,000 prospects. You'll have to consider where those prospects are as well. How you reach them will depend on whether your business is strictly local (a car detailing service, for example), national, or Web-based.

- **Frequency** – The rule of thumb is that people need to hear your message seven or eight times before they recognize and remember your brand; so count on repeating your promotions. Ideally, your marketing campaign will involve reaching out to your current and prospective customers at least once a month to stay at the tops of their minds. You've now established you have to reach 2,000 prospects at least seven or eight times per year. You could do that with television commercials, but even local cable ads can easily cost more than what you'll make all year in sales. You could plan to tell 2,000 people about your new business exclusively at networking events, but you'd have to do that seven or eight times, which would give you no time to actually run your business! The key is to find the best mix of marketing tactics that will accomplish your goal.

- **Budget** – Set your marketing budget as a percentage of your sales goal. If your annual revenue goal is $60,000, allocate 5% or 10% of this figure—$3,000 to $6,000—to spend over the year. This may seem like a lot when you're just starting out, but consider that $3,000 a year equals just $250 a month for twelve months, which is much easier to manage. As your marketing efforts turn into sales, set aside a portion of your "new" income for future marketing campaigns. And remember, there are many ways to get the word out and trade for marketing exposure that don't cost you a penny. More on this later.

Exercise **Promotional components**

Based on the explanation in the three steps above, fill in the chart below with the promotional components of your marketing plan.

Number of customer orders needed	Average customer purchase	Reach (number of prospective customers)	Frequency	Marketing budget
	$			$

MARKETING MIX OPTIONS

You are well on your way to developing an effective marketing plan. It's not margarita time quite yet, though. Next, you have to decide which promotions you'll use as part of your marketing mix. There are many options available for getting the word out, each with its own benefits and drawbacks, which are outlined in the following table. Whether you're strictly a local business or you sell on a national level will also play a key role in determining the best strategy for you.

Marketing Tactic	Description	Advantages	Disadvantages	Cost
Advertising	Purchasing space in a broadcast or print network such as TV, radio, newspaper, etc.	Gains a wide audience in a targeted geographical area; venue can often provide creative services to help you create your advertisement.	It takes several ads to gain recognition, which can become costly for a start-up. Results are hit or miss.	$$-$$$
Direct mail	Sending postcards, flyers, etc., directly to your potential customers.	Focused messages to an interested audience can increase response rates. Can be done quickly.	Printing and postage can get costly. Response rates are often low (1-3%).	$ - $$
Public relations	Using local or industry publications to promote your business.	You can learn to write your own press releases. You can reach a wide audience.	Necessary follow-up with reporters can be time consuming. Final published story is often out of your control.	$
Co-branding	Partnering with related businesses to cross-promote each other's offerings.	Casts a wider net.	Takes time to establish a relationship to be sure you share the same values and have the same expectations.	$
Web marketing	Maintaining an online presence (Web site, search results, search engine advertising, links, etc.) to promote your business.	Enables you to provide more detail for customers than typically allowed in any other type of campaign. Can sell directly to consumer with an e-commerce system.	An effective Web site must be up to date, which can take time and require technical skills you don't have.	$-$$

E-mail marketing	Sending regular e-mail messages to a list of subscribers.	Can be self-published, saving time and money. Cost-effective, measurable, and lasting. Low-cost online services (such as Constant Contact) simplify this task and can tell you which e-mail messages got read, deleted, forwarded, etc.	Must follow best practices to avoid spam penalties. E-mail inboxes are becoming cluttered so your messages may not always get read.	$
Networking	Making face-to-face connections with potential customers.	Begins a personal relationship which can be developed over time and last a lifetime; many networking options available.	Time consuming. Timely follow-up is required to be successful (see our networking chapter for tips).	$-$$

An effective marketing mix for a start-up business might be:

1. Set up your Web site—keep it simple. All you need to start with is a description of your products or services and how to contact you. Don't wait to go out with a Web site that is perfect; that will cost you too much time. Instead, aim for a professional site that you can build as your business progresses.

2. Send an e-mail to your current list of contacts to announce that you've started your business. This could be a simple text e-mail or you could use an online system that lets you easily create professional e-mail messages or newsletters. (See our Toolkit section for our recommendation.) Remember that frequency is key, so plan on sending at least a monthly or quarterly e-mail to your current and prospective customers. This is where the concept of "nurture" marketing comes in; it's making sure you reach out to your prospective clients (of course, this means your current clients as well because you want their repeat business) at least once a month. Staying on your customers' minds is very important because you never know when they'll be ready to buy. And you want to be there when they are.

3. Send a "grand opening" press release to local news editors in the hopes of gaining some media coverage.

4. Attend networking events to make new contacts for your business and to build your e-mail distribution list.
5. Collaborate with other businesses and organizations to co-promote each other and leverage each other's networks—online and offline.

In Her Words

"If you don't toot your own horn, who will? Be proactive in alerting the media to your news. Display your press clippings in a frame for customers and prospects to see. Some people direct mail the clippings to their customers/prospects. Newsworthy topics include events, survey results, awards, grants, public speaking gigs, new products, and community involvement."

—Betty Galligan, founder/president, Newberry Marketing & Public Relations (www.NewberryPR.com)

These are all relatively low-cost solutions, which start getting the word out that your products and services are available. Once you understand the feedback and results these campaigns are having, you can start to spend marketing resources (your time and money) on these and other marketing campaigns targeting your audience.

The key is to determine where your customers already are, and try to get in front of them there. There is no sense placing an article or purchasing an ad in a local business publication if that publication does not reach your audience. Talk to potential customers to see how they would look for your product or service and make sure they can find your contact info in those places.

Bright Idea

Get free press

If you can establish yourself as a subject matter expert, the media will come to you to round out their stories. One way to do this is to work with a local business school to have marketing students conduct a survey of your target audience on current issues and opinions, then send these study results to the media. In addition to giving you some important feedback about your customers, it gives reporters something timely to report on; they're always looking for current, relevant news.

Remember, their goal is not to promote your business, but to report what is going on in the community or industry.

WHERE IN THE WORLD ARE YOUR CUSTOMERS?

If you've done your homework, you know who the target market is for your product or service. But where are they? Once you can answer that question, you'll know where to spend your resources when advertising or networking.

- Look on the Web sites of the networking groups in your area, which often list member directories. You're looking to see if the businesses complement yours. If you sell gourmet chocolate, a gift basket company might be a great match.
- Study magazines that are also aimed at your target market. Look for industry events, such as trade shows, that you might consider attending.
- Reach out to former employers and colleagues, letting them know about your new business venture.

COLLABORATIVE MARKETING

No matter what your business is, there are other businesses that complement your products or services. Even though you're selling something completely different, you have the same target customer. If you're a wedding planner, your customer is the bride. Other businesses with that same bride in mind include a bridal store owner, photographer, musician or DJ, invitation designer, printer, hair and makeup stylists, caterer, and florist. Contact these professionals to talk about how you can work together to leverage your marketing reach. You could include links to each other's Web sites, write articles for each other's newsletters, or split the cost of holding an event for your prospective customers.

Michelle: One of my favorite collaborations was with three other marketing firms who co-hosted an event just before Valentine's Day, titled, "For the Love of Money." The theme was "romancing your customers." We chose a trendy club downtown, and decorated the place with red and pink heart decorations and roses.

We had promoted it as a business workshop with networking; and by marketing to all four of our lists through e-mail alone, we sold all 200 seats within the first week. The four of us highlighted our different specialties—Web programming, graphic design, search engine marketing, and direct mail marketing. We shared our knowledge with the audience during the presentation, then mingled during a cocktail hour. It was a very successful way to cross-pollinate our networks. We all invited our clients and introduced them to the other presenters, and made some new contacts of our own. Since we shared the planning effort and expenses, it was very cost-effective, and less of a burden than if we had put on an exclusive event.

COST-EFFECTIVE WAYS TO MAKE AN IMPRESSION

Your goal in marketing your company is to get the word out about your offerings. If only it were that easy. Fact is, you're competing for your customer's attention against a steady stream of other companies who are doing the same thing. You have to present yourself in a way that is memorable, so your customers think of you when you're not standing right in front of them. Here are a few ways to do this without breaking the bank:

- Monthly mailing—That's right; the old-fashioned, snail mail kind of letter that arrives in the mailbox. Think about it: E-mail inboxes are stuffed and people aren't always plugged in. But a simple postcard or letter may get someone's attention as they're sorting through mail. Send Out Cards (listed in the Toolkit at the end of this chapter) is a convenient service for just this kind of marketing.
- Take a photo at a client meeting or event and send it to your client via postal mail as a reminder of the occasion.

A QUICK WRAP-UP

There are as many ways to market your business as there are stars in the sky. Just remember to choose wisely so you don't throw time or money into a black hole. If you've been posting flyers for six months and they haven't resulted in any business, try a different tactic. And don't forget to participate on our Web site to connect with women who have great ideas about how to tell the world you're open for business.

REFLECTIONS

What are three things you're taking away from this chapter?

1. _____
   _____
   _____

2. _____
   _____
   _____

3. _____
   _____
   _____

COACHING FOR SUCCESS

As you create your marketing plan, answer the following:

- What words, images and colors come to mind in creating your brand?

   _____
   _____
   _____

- What marketing strategies will you start with to begin moving towards your marketing and sales goals?

   _____
   _____
   _____

- How will you measure the success of each strategy?

   _____
   _____
   _____

TOOLKIT

Check out these resources to stoke your marketing idea engine.

Books

- *Permission Marketing: Turning Strangers Into Friends And Friends Into Customers,* by Seth Godin. Seth is the former Yahoo! executive who built a brand on the claim that mass marketing is dead and permission e-mail marketing is in. He has a blog, which is pretty well done, and a string of new books, but this one is a must-read for those confused about the best way to reach their target audience.
- *The Guerilla Marketing series* by Jay Conrad Levinson. The books in this series offer practical, down-to-earth advice based on time-tested principles and common sense. A few titles:
  - *The Guerrilla Marketing Handbook*
  - *Guerrilla Marketing for Free: Dozens of No-Cost Tactics to Promote Your Business and Energize Your Profits*
  - *Guerrilla Marketing Weapons: 100 Affordable Marketing Methods*
  - *Guerrilla Marketing in 30 Days*
  - *Guerrilla Marketing for Consultants: Breakthrough Tactics for Winning Profitable Clients*

Web sites

- Small Business Administration (www.sba.gov) walks you through each step of developing your marketing plan.
- Constant Contact offers e-mail marketing solutions that are simple and cost-effective. Learn more on Precision's Web site, or take the demo tour and get a free trial at Constant Contact.
- Easy Site (www.EasySite.com). Get your Internet presence started with a free Web site in as little as fifteen minutes. Using templates and following a terrific, quick demo, it's easy—really!—to build your own Web site. A free site has limited functionality, but you will be able to publish a news page, calendar, photos, videos, audio, and more. Additional low-cost monthly payment plans offer additional features.
- Web Monkey (www.WebMonkey.com). This site can get you comfortable speaking the language of the Web in no time. We especially like the HTML cheat sheet and the variety of Web site development and marketing articles.
- Precision Web Marketing—Michelle's team of Web experts offers low-cost and easy ways to promote your Web site. Go to www. PrecisionROI.com.

- United States Patent and Trademark Office is the place to go should you choose to trademark your company name. Go to www.uspto.gov/web/offices/tac/tmfaq.htm#DefineTrademark.

Other resources
- **Photo montage**—Create a photo montage of a client meeting or event. Include your company logo and the client's company logo, and/or images of relevant words, like "success," "achieve," or "thanks." Go to www.KodakGallery.com.
- **Send Out Cards**—No more going to the store to buy cards, then going to the post office to mail cards. This system makes it easy to stay in touch with your customers on a regular basis. You'll even receive reminders so no one gets forgotten. Check out www.SendOutCards.com/TheSassyLadies.
- **Marketing material**—Get custom business cards, brochures, and post cards printed at Vista Print, www.vistaprint.com.

Logo design template Web sites:
- www.LogoYes.com gives you access to more than 20,000 symbols and tools to design your own logo for as low as $99.
- www.TheLogoLoft.com has many options to help you design your logo or have it designed.
- www.LogoWorks.com has different designers who help you with your concept.

If you like The Sassy Ladies' logo, we would love to refer you to Susan Johnson (www.Partner4success.com) from California. She was just a pleasure to work with. We liked her menu-style offerings. Working with Susan was easy, quick, and cost-effective.

If you have a Web site and want to know whether it's effective and how it looks from your customer's point of view, contact Miriam Perry for a Web site review at Miriam@TheSassyLadies.com.

THE SASSY LADIES' WEB SITE RESOURCES
Thank you for purchasing The Sassy Ladies' Toolkit for Start-up Businesses. To show our appreciation, we're providing you access to an additional resource, free of charge, on our Web site at: www.TheSassyLadies.com/StartupChapter5.
- Back-of-the-Napkin Marketing Plan.
    A quick-and-dirty—but effective—plan on who your customers

are, how you'll reach them, and what will convince them to buy from you.

Enjoy!

CHAPTER SIX

SELLING YOUR PRODUCT OR SERVICE— AND YOURSELF

"Every business is built on friendship."
—Unknown

In this chapter, you'll learn how to:
- Develop your sales pitch.
- Find customers.
- Barter with confidence.
- Use e-mail marketing.
- Draft a sales agreement.

You may not have made a single sale yet. Or, you may have been selling, but just not at the level you'd hoped. Either way, this chapter will help you get going and growing. If you think of your first year in business as a journey, then the following information is the fuel that makes it all necessary—and possible.

It doesn't matter whether you are offering a product or a service, or whether you're an expert or an artist: you are a saleswoman. The very idea of selling, though, can cause mild anxiety in some and full-blown terror in others. It takes no small amount of confidence to look your prospect in the eye and state your prices. Understanding the sales process will help you master this part of running your own business.

A note about selling: It may seem obvious that you have to know *whom* you're selling to before you decide *how* to sell to them, but we've seen entrepreneurs put the cart before the horse, so to speak, with predictably disappointing results. Be sure you know who the target audience is for your product or service. (The feasibility chapter gives you direction in this area.) In addition to the prospective customers you've defined, you have the contacts you've made through network-ing and referral sources.

WHOM DO *YOU* TRUST?
People don't buy from companies. They buy from people. Think about your own buying habits. You buy an ironing board from Target

because you like the store layout, their prices are good, and they sell those yummy peanut butter-stuffed, chocolate covered pretzels. It isn't necessary for you to have a good feeling about the clerk ringing out your purchase. But when you have to spend big money, buying a house for example, you buy from someone who "gets" you. If the real estate agent doesn't listen to you and keeps showing you colonials when you want a contemporary, you're going to someone else. When you choose a personal service, like daycare, it isn't based on price; it's based on your trust in the provider.

When you're a one-person show, how you come across to your customers is the most important factor within your control. The old saying about having only one chance to make a first impression is strong wisdom. And when you consider that as much as 90 percent of face-to-face communication is non-verbal, you can understand why the image you portray is so important. Here are five ways to give the right impression:

- Make direct eye contact to show you are paying attention and that you have nothing to hide.
- Wear conservative, professional clothing. We would almost feel silly saying something so obvious, except that we've seen people show up for a meeting in flip-flops, or dress for a networking event looking like it was club night. Those 3 ½ inch red leather pumps with the ribbon ankle ties are darling, really, but not at 8:30 in the morning.
- Be polite. Ever meet someone who oozes charm? A large part of charisma is good manners. Don't interrupt. Say "please" and "thank you."
- Show interest in the other person. When you're talking with some-one else, ask her how her business is doing. You can learn a lot about your client when you stop talking and listen, and you'll be amazed at the cues you pick up that can help you learn what her challenges are that you might be able to solve. If you babble when you're nervous, learn to stop it.
- Remember that you are always "on." This is especially true if you live in a small town. You never know who you're going to bump into. Do not, ever, ever, ever, go to the supermarket in your spandex leggings and cropped T-shirt. Of course, you have the right to time off and to be comfortable. But when you run your own business, you become the face of that business. If you're most comfortable in spandex, please enjoy it in the privacy of your own home. (This is

good advice even for people who don't own their business, don't you think?) There is, as with every rule, an exception: If you're a personal trainer or an image consultant and you have the body your customers want, then that's advertising.

You buy shine

To understand how to sell, think about how you buy. What are you really buying when you choose your shampoo? They all clean your hair, so why not buy the cheapest? You select your hair care because you want to define your curls, add volume, smooth your hair, add shine, or protect your color. You're buying the benefit of a certain type of shampoo. How does that translate to you? Don't sell your product or service, sell the benefit your product or service provides. If you're an accountant, you help people keep more of their hard-earned money. If you're a personal chef, you help your customers make the most of the limited hours in their day and help them eat healthier.

Always remember the WIIFM factor: From your customer's perspective, it's always about What's In It For Me. Don't make them guess; tell them what you can do for them. If you sell a consumer service (that makes you a B-to-C, which means business-to-consumer), your customers are looking for someone:
- They can trust
- Who can make their lives easier
- To do something they don't have the time or skills for

If you sell a consumer product, your customers are at least looking for:
- Convenience
- Luxury
- Necessity

If you sell a product or service to other businesses (that means you're B-to-B, a business-to-business company), your customers want something that will help them build their businesses, and it may include any of the above characteristics.

FACE-TO-FACE SELLING

This is not where you hone a slick sales pitch about why your prospective customer should buy from you. This is where you prove you've listened to your customer, done your research, and can help solve one or more of her problems. It's often said in the sales industry that people don't like to be sold to, but they like to buy. Prepare for a meeting with your prospective client by thinking about what your meeting goals are: what you want your client to get out of the meeting, and what you want to get out of it. This preparation helps to clarify your purpose and helps you keep the meeting on target. Once you're in the meeting:

- Thank your prospective customer for taking the time to meet with you.
- Respect her time; don't go over the allotted meeting length. It's a good idea to practice what you have to say before your meeting to make sure you stay in the allotted timeframe—just be sure you don't come off sounding like you're reciting a spiel.
- Begin with the benefit you offer. Example: I'd like to show you how I can increase your sales by 30%. Or: I'd like to talk to you about how I can take the workload and stress of planning your next event off your hands.
- Set clear and realistic expectations. If you're a copywriter and one of your benefits is quick turnaround time, say it and be specific:

80

I can turn this brochure around in ten days. On the other hand, if the customer is looking for you to write a 24-page brochure in three days, don't say you can do it if you can't. Be honest. Offer an alternative: "That timeframe isn't possible, but I could have it to you in one week."

- No hard selling. No doubt someone has once told you, "If you decide to buy this from me today, I'll give you 10% off." Did that work? We didn't think so. Be clear and be honest, and don't make your client feel she's being bullied into buying. That's not a strategy for a long-term relationship. Save special deals for trade shows, where discounts are expected and appropriate.
- State your price and what it includes. If your $500 consultation fee does not include travel expenses, be sure to say so.
- Don't leave the table wondering whether or not you just closed a deal. Ask if you have a deal. Once you've gone through the benefits of your product or service, and you've answered your customer's questions, ask her, "Shall I send you an agreement with all the details?" or "Shall I write your order up?"

In Her Words

"The people whom I speak with realize they need help, but most are new to working with virtual assistants so they are a little apprehensive when they hear my rate structure. For these clients, in my Agreement to Provide Services, I offer them a three-month reduced hourly rate so they can experience the benefit of working with a virtual assistant. After the three-month period, we review the tasks that have been completed and the goals the business owner has been able to accomplish. At point my standard hourly rate is easily accepted."

—Linda Siniscal, Third Hand Secretarial Service, LLC
(www.YourExtraHand.com)

GETTING PAST "NO"

It will happen. You've stated the benefit to your customer, did meticulous research, made a killer presentation, and the customer smiled and nodded in all the right places. When you asked her if you could send her your agreement, she said, "No, I don't think so."

It's OK, don't panic, this is all part of the process. Act like a pro and be prepared by responding, "May I ask what's holding you back? I want to understand so I can be sure I've interpreted your needs correctly." If she says the price is too high, ask her what a better price would be.

If she says she has to see other vendors, ask her when she expects to have made a decision. And don't be afraid to ask, "Have you met with anyone besides me? How did they compare?" Your goal here is to find out exactly what the barrier is so you can address it. Again, you don't want to come off as pushy—or desperate. You want to appear confident that you can work things out to create a win-win situation.

NEGOTIATION

You may be in a position to negotiate your prices. If you know what your profit margin is, you know how low you can go. For some businesses, a bit of wiggle room is built into the rates. However, in some cases, the price is the price. Whatever your approach, don't casually underprice yourself. These are just a few reasons not to accept lower than your standard rates:

- You're new in business and you're eager to get new clients.
- You're doubting if you're worth that much.
- You really want this sale.

The problem with these reasons is you're not thinking like a businessperson. You're thinking like some pitiful waif who has nothing of value to offer the world and should be grateful for the meager crumbs she's thrown. Get real! You are a competent, strong woman who had the vision and courage to start your own business. If a friend of yours was in your situation, you know darn well you'd give her the pep talk of the year to convince her she was worthy. Do the same for yourself. Or call your friend for that pep talk.

If someone asks you to lower your price and you feel you're already offering a fair price, say so. You might say:

- My rates (or prices) are not negotiable. Tell me what your budget is and I'd be happy to provide services (or product) for that price. (In other words, reduce the amount of service or product you're offering, don't reduce your price.)
- My rates are standard for the level of service and quality I'm offering. Do you think you'd be in a better position next quarter? I'd be happy to follow up with you then.
- My rates are relative to my experience. Perhaps you're looking for someone at a more junior level? I might be able to recommend someone. (The implication: You get what you pay for. If you want the best, you hire me. If you're looking for a bargain, you're at the wrong level.)

But, we can hear you saying, how can I get to a win-win? Ah-h-h, we're so glad you asked; read on.

BARTERING

There are times when you can—and should—work out a deal where your customer pays less in cash but you don't accept less in value. Bartering is when you trade similar items of value, rather than pay face value. This is terrific when you're first starting out. It's a way to build your portfolio and make contacts while getting something in return you can't afford just yet. Bartering can be a great solution even after you've become established. It's an acceptable practice among small businesses; opportunities to barter are limitless. Just a few examples:

- Advertising space for graphic design work
- Marketing consultation for business coaching
- Event planning for legal advice
- Web design for interior design consultation

The most important consideration when developing a barter is to be sure you are trading equal values of service or product. You don't want to feel as though you're being taken advantage of or that you're getting more than you're giving. If your hourly billing rate is $90 per hour, then you should be receiving $450 worth of product or service if you're offering five hours of service. A written agreement is a must to ensure both parties have the same expectations.

As wonderful as bartering is, remember that it's a short-term solution. You're in business to make money, after all.

PRO BONO WORK

There are times when it makes sense to work for free, otherwise known as *pro bono*:

- When a volunteer project allows you to pick up experience you need to round out your current skill set.
- When you're looking for a community service project that gives you the opportunity to share your talents for a good cause.
- When a pro bono project gives you the opportunity to work with people you normally wouldn't have a chance to meet.

These situations don't address the new college graduate or someone who is looking to switch careers. If you're reading this book, chances are you already have the skills and are looking to leverage your experience into your own business. If you've been working for someone else for years and are ready to go out on your own, you don't need to prove yourself. Save pro bono work for when you can afford to do a volunteer project.

Of course, all of this is not to say that volunteering your services just for the sake of contributing to your community isn't a great idea. Just be sure you're clear on why you're committing your time.

SOURCES OF WORK

In addition to finding clients through networking, you can find project work through temporary staffing agencies, company job boards, staffing boards, or online communities.

While taking a project through one of these resources could be lucrative and even turn into repeat business, a word of caution is in order. We've seen some extremely low rates on these job boards. On some auction sites, people are offering ridiculously low fees, known as low-balling, for the chance to win a project. This might be a good strategy for:

- College students who need to develop their skills and get as much experience as possible.
- People who have no experience in the field.
- Professionals from countries where the cost of living is extremely low.
- People who don't need money and are working just for fun (we suspect this is an incredibly small number).

The problem with low-balling is it sets unrealistic expectations on the employer's part, which, in turn, makes it difficult to earn a decent living. While there may be a short-term benefit to working for a pittance, we don't recommend it; there are just too many disadvantages. It's not easy to substantially raise your rates; a 5% to 10% increase is a lot to ask for. The perception that you get what you pay for can work against you if you're charging a very low rate. Plus, you're losing money when you don't get paid what you're worth. If you've worked for someone else, you have an idea of what your skills are worth. If not, do a little research to find out the salary range for someone in your business who's working for someone else. Use that information as a base for your fees. The fact that you're now in business for yourself should in no way translate to you making less money than you would if working for someone else. (Learn more about setting your prices in our feasibility chapter.)

SELLING ONLINE

A Web site is essential. At the very least, it's an online business card where prospective and current clients can find out how to contact you. At the other end of the spectrum, a Web site can exponentially increase your business. A thorough discussion of how to choose and reserve a Web domain name (your Web address), how to design an effective Web site, and how to manage a Web site is a book in and of itself. So, we're just going to cover a few points that relate directly to the topic of selling. Your Web site should:

- **Be professional**.
  - ○ The text on your Web site must be easy to read. No typos.
  - ○ All graphics must be relevant to the copy. This means: Unless you are a photographer, you should not have pictures of your children on the site. We can imagine how adorable the little tykes are, but this is not the place for your personal photo album. Same goes for your puppy, kitten, or vacation pictures. It is better not to have any graphics than to have graphics that are of poor quality or irrelevant subjects.
  - ○ Keep the design simple. Black or dark-grey text on a white background. No flashing icons. No music (unless you're a composer).
- **Think about your customer**.
  - ○ Everything on your site should be directly relevant to the questions a person considering your products or services would have. Do they want to see samples? Do they want to know what other people have said about your business (known as testimonials)? Do they have to know your prices?
- **Make it easy to contact you**.
  - ○ Your contact information should be at the bottom of every page or at least available from a Contact Me button in the main menu of your Web site. If you want people only to call you, then just list your phone number. If you would prefer everyone to e-mail,

just list that address. If you don't have a preference, list your postal address, e-mail address, telephone number, and fax number.

SELLING BY E-MAIL

We just said it's essential to have a Web site, didn't we? Of course, that doesn't mean you're going to go right out and get one if you don't already have one, does it? Regular e-mails from you are a professional option while you're working on your Web site, which could take as long as six months.

If you do have a Web site, you can drive people to the site to buy. If you don't have one, you can provide them with enough information to call or e-mail you with orders or requests for more information.

Using simple, permission-based e-mail news campaigns, you can reach out to all those you meet in your networking events on a regular basis, providing them with information such as:

- Activity surrounding your business.
- Information they might find useful or entertaining.
- Clarification on the types of products or services you provide.
- Notice of sales, specials, or upcoming events you plan to attend (This is a good opportunity to cross-promote other organizations' events—they will likely return the favor when you need the help).
- Examples of your happy customers—testimonials, case studies, success stories.

Your goal is to show that you exist, are active, and doing well. Project an image of success, and success will be attracted to you. Your intention is to build a relationship with every one of those people represented by the business cards in your contact file.

Using an e-mail application such as Constant Contact (whom the Sassy Ladies recommend; see our chapter on marketing), you'll be able to see who nibbles on your news, and can follow up accordingly. For example, if you send a news tip to one hundred people, and five of them reply with a nice note thanking you for the information, you might consider calling them in the next month. Perhaps one or two recipients will ask a question to clarify how the information applies to their business. Call or e-mail these people immediately—you've just identified a new prospect! Your one newsletter kick-started the sales process with an otherwise dormant contact. That's a great feeling.

The key is permission. Give people the option to hear from you regularly by getting their permission (in the form of their providing contact information to you). An opt-out or unsubscribe feature at the bottom is not just a nicety—you must have this by law (the CAN SPAM Act of 2003). Provide news and tips of interest to list-subscribers, and you'll have the opportunity to reach out to them about your company for months to come.

Bright Idea

Add your friends and family to your e-mail list—they are usually among the first to acknowledge your e-mail and forward it to others who might be interested in subscribing.

HOW TO CREATE AN E-MAIL NEWSLETTER

There are two ways to create an e-mail newsletter; here are the pros and cons for each.

Method	How it works	Pros	Cons	More Information
Do-it-your-self.	Create a regular e-mail using your e-mail software (e.g., Yahoo!, Microsoft Outlook, etc.)	• Very easy to create. • No added expense.	• If you're not careful, these messages can look unprofessional. • It can be difficult to manage your address book. • You have no way of knowing who opened the e-mail and whether they clicked to your Web site.	http://office.microsoft.com/en-us/templates/default.aspx
Web-based service	For a monthly fee, you use this service to create and manage your e-mail newsletter.	• Templates provide a professional look and are easy to read • Tracking tools let you see who opened your e-mail and which links they clicked	• It's an additional expense (but a small one, based on the size of your list)	www.ConstantContact.com

CONTRACTS AND AGREEMENTS

Working without a contract is like a high-rise window washer working without a safety line. Chances are nothing bad is going to happen, but why take the risk? A contract, or a simple agreement, gets everyone on the same page and clarifies expectations. It also projects you as the professional you are. A contract or agreement should do the following:

• Defines the work you will do.

- Sets the price for that work, along with additional fees for extra services.
- Establishes a timeline for the project, including when payment is due.
- Explains what will happen if the project is cancelled; specifically, how much you will be paid.

You can ask other professionals in your field to share the agreements they use, but we urge you to hire an attorney to be sure you have a contract or agreement that protects you and minimizes your risk.

Not selling: pulling the plug

Sometimes, saying no to a prospective client is the best thing you can do. We know the idea of not taking in new business seems to contradict the entire premise of this book and The Sassy Ladies in general. But, there are times when you will be better off not doing business with someone. It's not something you decide with a formula or spreadsheet. This is where one of your greatest gifts comes into play: women's intuition. It's the gut feeling you get when something isn't quite right. Heed this feeling. Know how, in the past, you ignored your intuition and then regretted it? Learn to listen. If there's something about the client or the deal that causes you pause: walk away.

The Sassy Ladies Say

Michelle: A prospect kept asking us to do design work, to demonstrate our style if we got the job. After indulging him with some preliminary e-mail designs, I got "that feeling" that he was going to take our creative ideas and try to use them himself, so I told him I preferred to sign a deal before completing any more work. When he pushed back, I held firm that we were not going to do any more work without a contract and a deposit. In the end, we ended up walking away from the project, because we did not feel he valued our time or was acting in a professional manner. I think he was trying to be the hard-as-nails negotiator, to establish himself in the relationship as the "top dog." When we walked away, he scrambled back a little bit, but the damage was done. My team no longer trusted (or liked) him, and I was too sassy to turn back!

Wendy: I met with a woman who asked to meet with me regarding the prospect of executive coaching. At the end of the meeting, when it was time to discuss cost, she said she had sticker shock. I knew then if she did hire me for coaching, her expectations would be way out of line. A year later, I saw her at an event and she acknowledged the price was fair. In fact, she had hired a coach who specialized in her industry and was paying even more than I quoted. I was happy that I didn't feel compelled to lower my rates—and the experience confirmed to me that my rates are in the right range.

Miriam: A prospective client wanted me to write copy for her Web site. My job was to convince people to donate money to her cause. I just didn't feel right about it; her cause seemed like a scam to me even though she had paperwork that was supposed to prove its legitimacy. I lost sleep thinking about how I might be responsible, even indirectly, for cheating people out of their money. It wasn't worth it. I politely declined, explaining that I already had a full workload (which was true, though I would have fit this project in if I felt better about it). I finally got a good night's sleep. And the next day—I kid you not—an existing client offered me a new project that equaled the exact amount of money I had lost by turning down the other project. I took that, and my clear conscience, as a sign that I had done the right thing.

REFLECTIONS

What are three things you're taking away from this chapter?

1. _____
   _____
   _____
2. _____
   _____
   _____
3. _____
   _____
   _____

COACHING FOR SUCCESS

As you define your dream, answer the following:

- What do you see as the most important challenge for you in the area of selling?

   _____
   _____
   _____
   _____

- What have you learned from others selling goods and services to you?

   _____
   _____
   _____
   _____

- What factor, such as a lack of self-confidence, may be affecting your ability to successfully sell your product or service and how can you overcome it?

   _____
   _____
   _____
   _____

TOOLKIT

Check out these resources to help you sell more successfully.

Books

- *Never Eat Alone: And Other Secrets to Success, One Relationship at a Time* by Keith Ferrazzi and Tahl Raz. Nurture relationships with key people to ensure your success and theirs. Michelle heard Keith speak at an event, during which he suggested categorizing contacts into three groups:
  - A-list—People you know very well and are likely to refer business
  - B-list—Those who need to be cultivated to send you referrals
  - C-list—Everybody else
- *How to Become a Rainmaker: The Rules for Getting and Keeping Customers and Clients* by Jeffrey J. Fox. This easy read gives common sense (which isn't so common) about selling and following up with customers.

Magazines

- *Selling Power*—Geared primarily toward sales management teams, but anyone who sells can benefit from much of the material. Go to www.SellingPower.com for subscription information, free articles, and e-newsletter.

Web sites

- **Constant Contact**—E-mail marketing made simple and, yes, fun! Take a tour and test drive a 60-day trial at www.ConstantContact.com.
- **Barter Bing**—An online bartering community (www.BarterBing.com) that lets you "barter the things you have for the things you want."
- **www.elance.com**—A job board geared toward Web developers, designers, writers, and other professionals.
- **www.CraigsList.com**—Online classified ads.
- **www.JustSell.com**—Free newsletters and articles focus on the nuts and bolts of selling. Very useful to develop and improve your selling strategy.

CHAPTER SEVEN

NETWORKING

*"Call it a clan, call it a network, call it a tribe, call it a family.
Whatever you call it, whoever you are, you need one."*
—Jane Howard (1533–1593), Countess of Westmoreland

In this chapter, you'll learn how to:
• Network with flair.
• Choose networking groups that suit you best.
• Make productive contacts.

Whether you begin networking as the next step in the process of getting your business off the ground or you're already out there, this chapter will help you make the most of your efforts. If you're new to networking, it will get you started on the right foot. If you consider yourself a pro, you can pick up a few new tips and get a refresher course on the underlying philosophy that makes some people so successful in their networking endeavors. If you think of your first year in business as a journey, then this chapter helps you find all those people along the trip who get you to where you're going.

True or false? Networking is a great way to make contacts, generate leads, and get new business. Actually, that was a trick question because the answer is: it depends. Whether networking is good for your business depends on how effective you are at not selling yourself. Yes, at not selling yourself; that wasn't a typo. The key to fruitful networking is to avoid the mindset that you're going to waltz into an event, work the room, trade as many business cards as possible and, as a result, you're going to get customers. Successful networking is about building relationships and, as with any satisfying relationship, it's a long-term situation. It's not like going out and picking flowers … it's more like planting seeds, which require time and nurturing to blossom.

Networking, by definition according to Merriam-Webster Online, is "the cultivation of productive relationships for employment or business." A productive relationship is a two-way relationship. If you approach networking as the chance to form a connection with someone you can help as much as someone who can help you, you'll be much more successful.

This concept has been proven by Business Networking International (BNI), a networking organization that generated more than two billion U.S. dollars of business in 2007. Its motto is "givers gain," and its members' success in 37 countries and all 50 states in this country prove that effective networking is about connecting, not selling. (More about that group in just a bit.)

HELLO, MY NAME IS …

Your palms are sweaty, your neck is cold, your vision is blurry, and you can't remember your name. No, you're not having a menopause moment (yet); you're walking into a roomful of strangers. And every fiber in your being is telling you to run back to your car and go home. Wait. Take a deep breath. You can do this! All it takes is a little preparation and a little practice. Here's how to walk—with confidence—into a room filled with strangers.

BEFORE YOU GO:

- Read the day's headline news stories. This could provide you the chance to start—or stay in—a conversation.
- Practice your elevator pitch. (See Chapter 2 for a detailed explanation.) That way, when you're standing in front of someone you desperately want to charm, but all you can think is, "Do I have spinach in my teeth?" you'll at least be able to begin the conversation sounding polished. Resist the urge to ad lib. Say what you do and stop talking. That will give the other person a chance to ask you questions (and prevent you from babbling).
- Study the invitation or member list and make a note of people you want to meet or for whom you may have a potential referral or connection. For example, if you are a graphics designer and you see there's going to be a printer at the event, that's a connection that could prove profitable for both of you. Or, if you were talking recently with someone who is looking for a Reiki therapist and you see that person on the list, it's a wonderful way to help two other people connect. You may not get immediate business out of this connection, but we believe that what goes around, comes around. Plus, this gives you something productive to do and say instead of just standing near the buffet table feeling lost.
- If you're planning to meet a specific person, find out the latest news about her company or industry by Googling her and checking out her Web site. When you do meet, you can say, "I just love your Web

94

site; I especially enjoyed the section on …"

- Invite someone to go with you to play tag team. Tell each other whom you're hoping to meet and be prepared to introduce her when you come across that person: "Let me introduce you to my friend, Wendy, who is a business coach. She's a great person for you to know." Be there for each other in between mingling with other people, but don't be a clique. After all, you already know this person; you're here to meet other people.
- Put a stack of your business cards within easy reach, either in the front pocket of your jacket or an outside pocket of your handbag. You don't want to have to dig for your cards in your purse. That's as painful to watch as it is to do.
- Bring a pen and a small notebook that fits in your purse so you can write down to-do items or reminders.

Bright Idea

Bring a lanyard and name tag holder with you; tuck a few of your business cards behind your name tag and you'll always have them handy.

WHILE YOU'RE THERE:

- When someone is talking to you, really listen. Not just with your ears, but with your whole body. Make and keep direct eye contact. Face her squarely. Be as interested in what she's saying as though she is the only other person in the room. Don't keep eyeing the door to see who else is walking in. It's distracting to the other person and it gives the impression you're waiting for someone more interesting to come in. Mother's advice rules here: treat the other person as you want to be treated.
- Make it your goal to find out how you can help your new contact promote her business; chances are she will reciprocate.
- Introduce yourself even if you know the other person's name, in case she forgot yours: "Hi Sue, I'm Mary Jones from ABC. We met at the Starlight fundraising dinner last month."
- When meeting someone for the first time, repeat his or her name throughout the conversation to help lock it into your long-term memory.

- If you go alone and no one's initiating contact with you, look for someone standing by himself, go over and introduce yourself. He'll be relieved to have someone to talk to. Ask him how often he attends these meetings. We know, on paper this sounds like a bad pick-up line, but everyone who attends networking meetings is there for the same reason: to meet people with whom they might do business. Just don't ask what sign he is, unless you're an astrologer.
- Small talk is a big challenge for some people. Once you get past the "what is your business" question, ask "feel good" questions that get people talking about themselves. A few examples to get you started:
  ◦ What inspired you to start your business?
  ◦ What do you enjoy most about what you do?
  ◦ What's the best thing anyone has ever said about your product or service?
- Don't forget—the average person knows 250 people. If you develop a relationship where people know you and trust you, it's six degrees (or less) of separation in action.
- Use the business cards you receive to write down reminders for you to follow-up on. For example, you might strike up a conversation with someone who would love to have the name of that grocery delivery service you've raved about. Ask for that person's business card and say, "Let me just make a note to send you that info so I don't forget" and write your reminder on the back of his or her card. People will appreciate you making such an effort to help them out. (Use your notebook to make these notes when a person's business card is glossy or too dark to write on.)
- Avoid staying with the same person for the duration. Always have three or four phrases to excuse yourself from a conversation, which is appropriate when someone is monopolizing your time or there's someone else you want to talk to. After your exit phrase, shake the other person's hand, which is a firm, but polite, signal that you're leaving. For example:
  ◦ "It was great to see you. There are a few other folks I need to connect with. Enjoy the event."
  ◦ "There's Michelle. She's a Web marketing expert; let's go say hi." Introduce the two and make your exit.
  ◦ "I need to find the ladies' room. It was good to meet you." If you don't feel comfortable giving that much detail, just say, "I need to excuse myself. It was nice to see you."

- Speaking of handshakes, make yours a solid one. Don't be a wet fish. This is no time to be dainty. Firmly grasp the other person's hand, look him in the eye, and say, "It's great to meet you." Say it, and shake it, like you mean it. A weak handshake is a sign that you either don't care or you don't have confidence in yourself, neither of which is a good signal when you're trying to convince someone he should do business with you. If you're not sure whether your handshake is firm, practice with a friend. Trust us; this is worth doing.

Bright Idea If you've forgotten someone's name, don't waste your energy trying to remember it; it's all you'll focus on during your conversation. Just come right out and admit it. You could try a little humor: "I'm so sorry, I have name amnesia; my doctors are working around the clock to help me. Please remind me of your name." It happens to everyone and people will admire your forthright, but diplomatic, way of handling a potentially awkward situation.

Share your favorite line on our blog or networking discussion board at www.TheSassyLadies.com.

AFTER THE EVENT

- Write the date and name of the event on the back of each business card you received. Also make a note about topics you discussed, which will be an icebreaker the next time you meet and gives you an opportunity to make contact again. You could send a brief e-mail message such as, "It was great to meet you last week at the Chamber event. I enjoyed our conversation about business development. I came across the attached article on the same topic and thought you might be interested."
- Follow up. This is an often overlooked, but extremely important, step. Whether it's a business connection or a recipe, your follow-up shows that you're true to your word and there's no better impression you can make than that.
- If you have an e-newsletter, send it to your new contacts with an intro such as: "It was great to meet you at yesterday's networking event. I think you might be interested in my e-newsletter, which provides financial tips for small businesses. You should be getting the next issue in about a week or so. If you'd prefer not to receive it, simply unsubscribe."

How to Evaluate Which Organizations to Join

Some networking groups are geared towards women, some are region or industry-specific, some are more social, while others are highly structured. Find out before you join a group if it's the right fit for you. It's your responsibility to do your homework. That guarantees that you'll not only get the business you're looking for, but that you'll be able to provide others with strong referrals, which can only help you. Don't go by price alone. Here are a few questions to ask current members. Introduce yourself, let her know you're new and ask if she'd mind a few questions. These are also great icebreaker questions.

- What motivated you to join this group?
- How are the meetings structured?
- How long have you been a member?
- What do you like best about this group?
- If you could change one thing about this group, what would it be?
- What percentage of your business is a result of your membership in this group?
- Is it easy for you to provide referrals to the other members?
- What other groups do you belong to?

You can ask these questions in person or through e-mail if you've already made contact with the person and she's offered to answer your questions. No matter how you ask, just be sure you do. You're not being pushy or nosy. You're being savvy about your time, energy, and money, which—in addition to being personal resources—are now your business resources as well. Don't forget: Everyone was new to networking at one time, they remember what it was like, and they're happy to help you get started.

To Find Out About the Networking Groups in Your Area:

- Conduct an Internet search. Use the phrase *business network* and your state. For example: Texas business network.
- Check your state's economic development or government Web site (for example, in Rhode Island those would be, www. EveryCompanyCounts.com and www.ri.gov, respectively).
- Ask the alumni services office of your high school or college if they have a listing of networking groups in the area. You should also check out the alumni networking events.

- Contact your local Chamber of Commerce. You can join any Chamber, but probably will be best served by one that is either local to you or representative of your ideal customers.

Most organizations will let you visit an event or two before you make the decision to join. Take advantage of the opportunity to talk with current members and to find out about the types of events that are held throughout the year.

A FEW NETWORKING GROUPS TO CONSIDER:

Organization	Factors to consider	Networking structure	Why you might prefer this group	Learn more
Chambers of Commerce	You can join any Chamber. You might choose your local chapter to cultivate clients in your community. Plus, events will be near your home (or office).	Monthly networking events (such as Business After Hours) are usually scheduled at the end of the day.	Chamber events are highly social. The more involved you are with committees and events, the better known you'll become.	See www. uschamber. com/chambers/directory for Chambers by state.
Business Networking International (BNI)	Attendance is mandatory. If you miss more than the allowed number, your membership will be terminated. Weekly meetings are usually held early in the morning, before the start of the work day, though there are a few lunchtime groups.	Meetings are highly structured and include open networking followed by each member describing his or her business to the group. Members are encouraged to hold one-on-one meetings to get to know more about each other's businesses.	The structured nature of the meetings means you don't have to face a roomful of strangers. In fact, because you get to know each other so well, it's like seeing a group of your friends each week.	See www. bni.com for information about the organization and a list of chapters in your state. Note that only one industry representative is allowed in each chapter (i.e., one freelance writer, one business coach, one Web marketer).

Women's business centers	In addition to networking events, these groups offer classes (some free) to help you start and grow your business.	Varies by group	The contacts you're likely to make with these centers are invaluable and long-lasting.	www.sba. gov/services/ counseling/ wbc/serv_ cnsling_wbc. html
National Association of Women Business Owners	Chapters are available in most metropolitan areas. National events expand your contacts.	Varies by chapter	In addition to providing education and networking opportunities, this group is an advocate in state and federal policy making for issues that affect women entrepreneurs.	www.nawbo. org

OTHER GROUPS THAT MAY SERVE YOU WELL:

- Executive Women's Golf Association—Golf is as much a business tool as it is a sport. This group helps women learn to master the game and the business aspects. No golf experience is necessary to join; see www.ewga.com.
- Local groups—These are the toughest to find because their presence varies widely by location. The best way to find them is to start with more formalized and well-known organizations like those mentioned above and ask around. Examples in Rhode Island are:
  - ○ Entrepreneurship Forum of New England—connects entrepreneurs through events and online communities; also offers team membership, which provides you with a focused board of advisors to coach and guide you to achieve your business goals. Check out their Web site at www.efne.org.
  - ○ Rhode Island Women's Network—a monthly meeting where members and visitors get together to hear a brief presentation showcasing a member's expertise, followed by dinner and networking. Visit the Web site www.riWomensNetwork. com for schedule, location, fees, and member directory.
  - ○ Center for Women and Enterprise—serves women entrepreneurs in Rhode Island and Massachusetts through events and workshops that are often free or very affordable. Check out

www.cweonline.org.
- The Sassy Ladies' networking events—check out the News page of our Web site for a list of where The Sassy Ladies will be networking. Come join us—we'd love to meet you there!
- U.S. Small Business Administration (SBA)—an independent agency of the federal government, this group supports small businesses by providing free or low-cost counsel, programs, and resources. Local offices operate as Small Business Development Centers (SBDC). Learn more about the SBA at www.sba.gov; find your local SBDC office at www.sba.gov/localresources/index.html.
- Toastmasters International—helps its members become better speakers and listeners in a fun and supportive environment. Find out more at www.toastmasters.org.

The wonderful thing about networking is that most people are happy to help you get started, because they know what it's like to be where you are. And someday, you'll do the same for someone else, won't you?

In Her Words

"BNI gets people out and about meeting each other. Every member has an opportunity to stand up each week, give a sixty-second infomercial on who they are and the kind of client they're looking for. Because we allow only one person per profession in each chapter, members have twenty-nine other business professionals who are listening for the ideal referral for them. BNI has had a tremendous impact in the small-business community."

—Patti Salvucci, Director of the Greater Boston Area Business Networking International (BNI), (www.bni.org)

Hear the full interview with Patti on our Web site.

The Sassy Ladies Say

Michelle: When evaluating groups to commit your resources to, consider where the majority of your clients are likely to be members.

Wendy: Different groups can serve different needs of your business. When I first started in business, I loved BNI because it also helped me find resources that I needed for my own business such as CPAs, attorneys, graphic designers, etc. Nine years later, I am involved with other groups in other geographic locations.

Miriam: Re-evaluate your networking group options every year. Your needs—and schedule—change. You might also benefit from getting involved with different groups over time.

SOCIAL NETWORKING

Listen, girl. Now that you're in business, you're going to need your social network for more than just becoming homecoming queen. This form of marketing, especially within online communities, is growing in popularity for business purposes, too. In the not-too-distant past, you might have only gone to Facebook or MySpace to check out the girl your son was taking to the prom, or to find yourself a date for next weekend. Many folks still consider these sites primarily for personal use, or even fear them as unsafe places where predators lurk. But a few popular sites are quickly becoming a great way to connect with business people and promote yourself from the comfort of your own desk.

The online reference Web site Wikipedia.org defines a social network service as that which "focuses on the building and verifying of online social networks for communities of people who share interests and activities, or who are interested in exploring the interests and activities of others, and which necessitates the use of software. Most services are primarily Web-based and provide a collection of various ways for users to interact, such as chat, messaging, e-mail, video, voice chat, file sharing, blogging, discussion groups, and so on."

While we're still in the early stages of seeing how these sites are useful for business purposes, we Sassy Ladies are embracing the concept. Until recently, the Web was only useful for organizations to connect to each other through their Web sites. With the dawn of social network sites, individuals can post their own Web pages in the form of profiles, photo albums, even videos and audio files, and can connect to others easily and inexpensively. This presents a great opportunity for you to reach out to those who can help you in your business—customers, prospects, partners, vendors—all by surfing the 'Net; whether you have a Web site yet or not.

Here are some ways you can use social networks in your business efforts:

- **To learn**—It is our goal for our very own Sassy Ladies' Web site to become a community for women entrepreneurs across the globe, a place to interact, connect, and share ideas and wisdom with other women who want to start and grow their businesses. You can learn from the stories of other women through our podcast interview series. You can post questions and answers on our Web site, and connect with women who may be important to your success through our community section. You can get tips from the blog and add your own comments. There are many such Web sites available and you can expect to see more and more cropping up as the technology becomes mainstream.

- **To connect**—Many sites help connect you with the people you know or with people you don't know, but with whom you have things in common. We've created our own profiles in MySpace and Facebook, but at the time of this writing, we've had better business experiences with our LinkedIn.com profiles. On this site, you can post a professional profile, link to your Web site, and showcase the people in your network whom you trust. While you can search for people by name, profession, region, or even keyword, you cannot connect with them unless they are linked through your network. (Think six degrees of separation; it's the same concept, but you can only see two degrees—those connected to you (first degree contacts), and those connected to them (second degree). We've enjoyed finding former colleagues and facilitating connections among our peers through this easy to use (and free!) Web site. It's a great way to follow-up with someone you've had a one-on-one networking meeting with so you can stay connected.
- **To contribute**—add your own knowledge to sites such as Wikipedia. com. By sharing what you know (and providing links to your Web site or e-mail address, if allowed) you increase your footprint on the Web and it can be a great way to promote your business.

You'll want to use caution with posting personal information, of course. And, use your best discretion with the photos, text, and other information you post to your profile. You might think it's fun to show the world that photo of you and your girlfriends doing shots at the bachelorette party, but do you really want your prospective client seeing that side of you? You want to maintain a professional appearance at all times online, just as you do offline. So, relax, have fun, and go make some connections!

ONE-ON-ONE MEETINGS

Whether or not you join a formal group, be proactive in networking and relationship building. Act with the intention of not only getting your name out there, but meeting people you can refer business to. In addition to contributing to the what-goes-around-comes-around philosophy, your ability to provide your potential clients with contacts they need will increase your value to them. One-on-one meetings are an important step in building relationships with your network. As in any solid relationship, it's give and take so be sure to make your one-on-one meetings as much about the other person's business as it is about yours. Your objective is to learn how you can help each other, and when you come from that mindset, you not only set good karma in motion, you'll get better results.

a. Find people who complement your business. For example, if you're a mortgage consultant, a real estate attorney would be a good complement. To find professionals in this field look in the phone book, conduct an Internet search such as "Oregon real estate attorney," or check the member directory of networking organization Web sites.

b. Call or e-mail them (see sample e-mail at the end of this chapter) to introduce yourself and ask for a face-to-face meeting so you can find out more about each other's businesses. Be sure to offer to buy coffee, if not lunch.

c. During the meeting, explain that as you meet people in the course of your business, you want to develop a network of people to whom you can refer your clients for dependable and excellent service. Questions to ask to find out more about the other person's business include:

- Tell me about your business (this seems like a no-brainer, but the simplest questions are the best).
- How did you get started in your business?
- What inspired you to go into business for yourself?
- Describe your ideal client.
- What kind of clients aren't good for your business?
- How do you prefer clients contact you (phone or e-mail, for example)?
- Ask for a few business cards so you can hand them out to potential clients.

d. Absolutely, positively, without exception you are to follow up with an e-mail or, even better, a handwritten note thanking the other person for his or her time. Set aside time each day to handle correspondence so you don't forget.

e. Whenever you meet someone who might be a potential client for someone else, offer to make an introduction via e-mail (see sample e-mail at the end of this chapter).

In Her Words

"I believe in creating synergistic circles to connect with people who are looking for a win-win situation. It's about creating and nurturing relationships, and being open to what the Universe sends you. This approach creates a powerful synergy that surrounds you in your business."

—*Linda Joy, editor, aspire …*
Magazine *(www.AspireMag.net)*

Hear the full interview with Linda on our Web site.

Exercise   **Identifying networking groups**

Choose a networking group, go to its Web site, look through the member directory, and list ten people you want to meet. Using the tips described in this guide, find out something about them, their business, or their industry that would help you break the ice in conversation. Or think of a referral they might appreciate. Now, register for at least one networking event for that group this month and network … with confidence, of course!

Name and Company	Fact or Referral

REFLECTIONS

What are three things you're taking away after reading this chapter?

1. _____

   _____

   _____

2. _____

   _____

   _____

3. _____

   _____

   _____

COACHING

Prepare for successful networking by answering the following questions.

- Describe the person you would love to meet at the next networking event.

   _____

   _____

   _____

- How will you introduce yourself?

   _____

   _____

   _____

- What keeps you from networking as much as you should?

   _____

   _____

   _____

- What will networking contribute to your business?

   _____

   _____

   _____

TOOLKIT
These networking resources will support your quest for win-win connections.

Books
- *Business by Referral: A Sure-Fire Way to Generate New Business* by Ivan Misner. A systematic approach along with handy tools to create strong, lasting business relationships. A valuable resource whether you're new to networking or an experienced veteran.
- *Endless Referrals, Third Edition* by Bob Burg. This book shows you how to: turn every contact into a sales opportunity, dramatically increase your business without spending more time or money, identify the most profitable contacts, network the Internet, set up a successful home-based business, take the intimidation out of telephoning, overcome fear of rejection, succeed in multilevel marketing and mail order marketing, position yourself as an expert, and mark yourself for success. (Description from amazon.com.)
- *Never Eat Alone: And Other Secrets to Success, One Relationship at a Time* by Keith Ferrazzi and Tahl Raz. An easy-to-read book that explains the best way to approach the art of networking: it's all in the title. A must for every businessperson's bookshelf.
- *Seven Second Marketing: How to Use Memory Hooks to Make You Instantly Stand Out in a Crowd* by Ivan Misner. Remember—and be remembered by—your best customers and referrers.
- *The Referral of a Lifetime: The Networking System That Produces Bottom-Line Results Every Day!* by Tim Templeton. An inspiring parable that explores the process and investment of developing a network of lasting business connections.

Article
- "The Importance of Being Memorable," an article by Scott Allen on five ways to help people remember you (Entrepreneurs.about.com).

Products
- Card scanners—Scan, categorize, store, and manage business cards in electronic files (www.cardscan.com).

THE SASSY LADIES' WEB SITE RESOURCES

Free additional resources on our Web site at www.TheSassyLadies.com/StartupChapter7.

- Networking Checklist
  Use this handy checklist to make sure you're prepared before you go and you're ready for action when you return.
- Networking Visualization Exercise
  If it works for Olympic champions, visualization will work for you, too! Let Wendy guide you to your perfect networking outcomes.

Enjoy!

APPENDIX A
E-mail samples

Introducing yourself

This is a sample of an e-mail you'd send to introduce yourself to someone.

> From: Miriam Perry
> To: Jared Banaca
> Subject: Introduction
>
> Hi Jared:
>
> You and I both attended last week's Chamber of Commerce Business After Hours event, but we didn't get to meet. As a freelance writer who specializes in developing Web site copy, I thought I might be of assistance to your clients for whom you are building Web sites. I know that Web design projects often come to a screeching halt because the client can't provide the copy the developer needs to move forward. At the same time, clients who want their Web sites redesigned sometimes start with me, and I'd like to be able to refer them to a Web design firm.
>
> Do you have time to meet next week so we can chat about our business models to see if we'd be good referrals for each other—perhaps Tuesday morning or Thursday afternoon for coffee?
>
> Best,
> Miriam

Introducing two people who haven't met

This is a sample of an e-mail you'd send to introduce two people you know.

From: Michelle Girasole
To: Paula M.; Jim G.
Subject: Virtual Introduction

Hi Paula and Jim:

Paula and I had a conversation at a luncheon yesterday in which Jim's real estate investment series came up. I offered to connect you two via e-mail.

Paula, an author and speaker whose radio show provides a weekly dose of financial inspiration, conducts workshops for corporations and other organizations.

Paula, meet Jim, creator of the real estate series I am speaking at in April. His events, which regularly sell out, seem a perfect partner to your financial management show.

I hope you two can connect soon.

Best regards,
Michelle

CHAPTER EIGHT

BUSINESS STUFF

"I've got a head for business and a bod for sin."
—Melanie Griffith as Tess McGill in Working Girl

In this chapter, you'll learn how to:
- Decide when to hire a lawyer and accountant.
- Determine what kind of insurance you should have.
- Find out what permits or licenses you need.
- Structure your business.
- Track your financial records.

This chapter on business stuff isn't necessarily the last step in the process of getting your business up and running. But many people leave it last because, and we're just being honest here, it's not as fun as the other steps. Unless your business is accounting, it's probably the last thing you want to think about. But think about it you must! If you think of your first year in business as a journey, then this is the part where you know the rules of the road so you don't get yourself into trouble. Even if you've started your business and haven't paid attention to the information in this chapter, it's never too late. Bite the bullet and do the right thing.

We've been told that one of our most charming attributes is our honesty. We tell it like it is—tactfully, of course. So, let's say what needs to be said, right here and right now: This is not the fun part of starting or running your business. But it is absolutely necessary. This is where you cross your T's and dot your I's so you don't lose sleep—or your business.

One of the tenets of success is being smart enough to hire your weaknesses. Unless you have a trust fund backing you up, being in business for yourself means learning to do lots of things yourself. But staying in business requires that you know which things are beyond you, and hiring the right people for the job.

111

A GOOD ACCOUNTANT IS A MUST-HAVE

If managing your taxes is like a man designing a comfortable bra (in other words, neither of you are in your element), then there's no question that you need to hire an accountant. It is as obvious a decision as buying your favorite shoes in black and brown. Now if you happen to be a financial whiz, then more power to you. If not, an accountant is one of the first people you want to consult so you can:

- Choose the best business structure, based on the specifics of your business. Your accountant will know whether you'll get a tax advantage as a sole proprietor, LLC, or corporation. (More on that in just a bit.)
- Be a lot less stressed at tax time. The time to see your accountant is not April 14. It's Day One of your business. This will minimize nasty surprises, such as finding out that you owe 15% self-employment tax.
- Be less stressed all year round. If balancing your checkbook turns you into a hair-pulling, cussing, muttering psychopath, let a bookkeeper handle your daily business finances.
- Find out what expenses you can claim as deductions. In addition to auto expenses, supplies, and business-related travel, you may be able to claim subscription and advertising fees, and more.

Most accountants offer a free consultation (if you find one that doesn't, find someone else). Use this opportunity to find someone with whom you feel comfortable. As is the case any time you hire someone, get a referral if you can.

LEGAL EASE

Lawyers aren't just for lawsuits. Hire a lawyer:

- To review contracts, agreements, or leases that you've been asked to sign or that you're asking your clients to sign.
- To help you secure a trademark or patent.
- If you're considering merging or partnering with another company, be sure the attorney has a background in small business so you'll get the right advice. Your state bar association or women's business center may have a referral—it's best to ask for someone who specializes in small business.

LICENSES AND PERMITS

What type of license or permit you need to run your business depends on the type of business and your state and city laws. A visit to your town hall may be all that's needed to get you the information you need for your business and locale.

Here are a few examples of the types of licenses you may be required to obtain:

This type of license:	Is required for/when ...
State license	Certain businesses depending on the industry or product being sold. Just a few examples: mechanic, cosmetologist, private investigator, real estate agent. You need a special license to sell certain products, such as alcohol, cigarettes, or gasoline.
Sales tax license or seller's permit	Retail sellers.
Employer registration	Businesses with employees
Federal permit	Certain businesses, such as financial investment firms, interstate trucking companies, etc.
Employer Identification Number (EIN), also referred to as a federal tax identification number	You have employees or meet IRS guidelines. You will also need this to set up your business checking account.
DBA (Doing Business As)	You're going to open a checking account under your business name.
Health permit	The sale of food items, which have to be prepared in a facility that meets health guidelines.

IN THE ZONE

Zoning is what determines how a given piece of property can be used. If you want to set up a retail store or you need an office or other type of business space, you have to choose a location zoned for that type of business. If you omit this step, the city or town government could close you down. Your visit to town hall should include a visit to the planning office, where you'll learn which zoning laws apply to you.

WHO ARE YOU?

Whether your business should be structured as a sole proprietorship or a corporation depends on factors that an accountant or tax attorney can best advise you on, but the following simplified descriptions of each type of business entity will give you an idea of which might work best for you. Do a little research (the reference librarian at your local library or a consultation with the Small Business Development Center can be fantastic resources) before you talk to an accountant or an attorney so you'll at least have a basic understanding and can use the meeting to validate what you do know and what you need to learn more about. For example, if you are considering becoming incorporated, you'll need to know what state to incorporate in, what type and how much liability protection you need, state fees, tax benefits, and whether you can file the necessary paperwork yourself. Also, be sure you know what's required to end a business because once you file legal papers, it might be a little more complicated than just tearing up your business cards.

Type	Description	Pros	Cons
Sole proprietor	Usually defined as a business that is owned and operated by one person, though the proprietor may have any number of employees. If you choose this legal structure then, legally speaking, you and your business are one and the same.	• It's easy • Sole ownership of profits • Flexibility • Control and decision-making authority vested in one person • Relative freedom from government control	• Unlimited liability • Instability— business could be crippled or terminated upon illness or death of owner • May be difficult to obtain financing • Income of the business is taxed to the proprietor
General partnership (general or limited)	An association of two or more people who carry on as co-owners of a business for profit.	• It's easy • Direct sharing of profiles among partners • Greater possibilities for financing and growth • Flexibility • Pass-through tax treatment	• No limit to personal liability • Elimination of any partner may constitute automatic dissolution of the partnership • Any partner can take action that legally binds the partnership as a whole • The individual partners and the business are a single entity for tax purposes
Corporation	One person may own all the stock of a corporation, and such person may be its only director and hold all required officer positions.	• Stockholder's liability has limitations • Ownership is readily transferable • The corporation continues to exist if a principal officer or owner becomes ill or dies • Relative ease in securing capital • Centralized control is secured when owners delegate authority	• Double taxation (C Corporation only) • Must adhere to corporate formalities, including local, state, and federal reports; must hold annual and special meetings; board of directors must approve material actions • Can be more costly to form and run than other business entities

*Provided by Rhode Island's Center for Women & Enterprise

Happiness is never having to say, "I'm not insured"

Before you hit the snooze button, grab a latte and listen up: Insurance is part of doing business the right way. This is not an area where you want to take your cousin Suzie Lou's advice—unless she's an insurance agent, accountant, or lawyer. Find out if you need, among others:

- Business interruption—A safety net in case you're prevented from doing business as usual because of a disaster (PMS is not considered a disaster—go figure).
- Malpractice insurance—Depending on your line of work, this will protect you against suits from clients who claim you didn't do your job.
- Liability insurance—Covers business-related injuries that occur on your property, such as your client falling out of his Hummer onto your driveway.
- Health insurance—For you or your employees.
- Workers' compensation, disability, and unemployment—All necessary if you have employees.
- Property insurance—Coverage for theft or damage caused by fire, flood, and other acts of God (or Goddess, if you so desire).

Getting certified as a minority or woman-owned business

Getting Women Business Enterprise (WBE) certification can be an advantage when bidding for business from corporate or government organizations. It's not a guarantee for getting new business, but it could be a foot in the door.

In addition to meeting other criteria, a woman owner must:
- Own at least 51% of the business.
- Have U.S. Citizenship or U.S. Resident Alien status.
- Contribute capital and/or expertise.
- Pay a non-refundable fee of $300-$450, depending on business location.

The certification process takes 60–90 days from the time you send in your application packet. Find out if this certification is right for your business at www.wbenc.org.

COPYRIGHT, TRADEMARK, AND PATENT PROTECTION

What's the difference between a copyright, trademark, and patent?

- **Copyright**—Used to protect original intellectual works, including literary, musical, and artistic. U.S. copyright laws are invoked from "the time the work is created in fixed form," according to the U.S. Copyright Office. For example, this book is copyright protected, which means only the authors have the right to sell, reproduce, or distribute this book. No special form or license is required. Learn more at www.copyright.gov.

- **Trademark**—According to the U.S. Patent and Trademark Office, a trademark is used to protect "a word, phrase, symbol or design, or a combination of words, phrases, symbols or designs, that identifies and distinguishes the source of the goods of one party from those of others." For example, Coca-Cola is a trademark. Go to www.uspto.gov for more information on the definition of a trademark, and to apply for one online.

- **Patent**—This type of protection is reserved for inventions and designs. The Snugli baby carrier is an example of a patented design. See www.uspto.gov to secure a patent online.

If you're still not sure which, if any, of the above you need, this is a great conversation to have with your attorney.

TRACKING YOUR FINANCES

How sophisticated do your financial records have to be? It depends on how complicated your business is. Your accountant can advise you on what type of records your business structure may have to keep by law. You may be able to use a simple spreadsheet, but it's a wise move to start using a software program such as Quicken or QuickBooks; you'll need it as you grow.

At the very least, you should be keeping track of your invoices, payments received, and expenses. See the end of this chapter for an income statement template.

Visit www.irs.gov, click the Businesses tab, then the Starting a Business link to learn about tax filing rules and dates.

In Her Words

"I started my business a few years ago because I wanted to use my education and passion for jewelry making and design. The creation part is my passion, the financial and business sides were not. Therefore, the most challenging part has been figuring out how to run the business side. Without a great system in place I didn't really get clear on how my business was doing until tax time! Having a system that gives you feedback helps you make changes along the way so you know what's working and what's not working."

—Renee Newton, jewelry designer
(www.PowderMillStudio.com)

REFLECTIONS

What are three things you're taking away after reading this chapter?

1. _____
   _____
   _____

2. _____
   _____
   _____

3. _____
   _____
   _____

COACHING FOR SUCCESS

As you go about taking care of the business details, answer the following:

• What business structure is the best fit for my business?

   _____
   _____
   _____
   _____

• Who can I ask for a referral to an accountant? An attorney?

   _____
   _____
   _____
   _____

• What is the next small step I can take toward formalizing my business entity?

   _____
   _____
   _____
   _____

TOOLKIT

Here are a few resources to help you get your business stuff done.

Books

Keeping the Books: Basic Recordkeeping and Accounting for the Successful Small Business by Linda Pinson—If you're going to try keeping your own books, this is a primer for preparing the necessary financial statements.

Web sites

- www.nolo.com—Read articles, follow step-by-step instructions, and get forms and templates to handle many legal issues without hiring an attorney. At the very least, it's a great reference to educate yourself about your particular issue before you hire an attorney.
- www.microsoft.com/templates—Download tons of templates for invoices, reports, project plans, presentations, and so much more—and they're all free.

THE SASSY LADIES' WEB SITE RESOURCES

Thank you for purchasing The Sassy Ladies' Toolkit for Start-up Businesses. To show our appreciation, we're providing you access to an additional resource, free of charge, on our Web site at www. TheSassyLadies.com/StartupChapter8.

- The Sassy Ladies' Time Tracker—Use this handy chart to track your hours, which is not only an effective time management tool, but can help you determine if the number of hours you're putting in to your business is consistent with your financial plan.

Enjoy!

EPILOGUE

We hope you've gained a nugget or three of wisdom between the covers of this book and that you've enjoyed taking this journey as much as we've enjoyed accompanying you on it. Get even more out of this book by revisiting it now and then. What you needed to know the first time you read it will be different than what you need to know the third time.

Beyond good advice, common sense, personal insight, and the basic business rules, the best thing you can do is to believe in yourself. You CAN do this. You CAN create a successful business. You CAN have the life you dream of. If you have to tape those words to your bathroom mirror, dashboard, closet door, washing machine (hey, whatever it takes to make that task less odious, right?), journal cover, jewelry box, or computer screen, do it. Even if you don't believe it, read it out loud until you do.

Please remember that no matter where you are in your business, there is no need to go it alone. Someone, somewhere, has been where you are now, whether that's a good place or a not-so-good place. And having been blessed with a double dose of the X chromosome, we are of the gender that enjoys sharing and collaborating. We know, that was a broad generalization (Get it? Broad? Are we hilarious or what?), but we're comfortable making it because many of you have shared stories that prove it. Come to our Web site, join our community, ask questions, share your story; in short, be inspired and be inspiring.

⟭

Visit us at www.TheSassyLadies.com.

Check out our free newsletter, join a discussion on our blog, hear other women share their insights, subscribe to our Club resources, and get our latest books and guides.